AN ILLUSTRATED HISTORICAL REVIEW OF THE MANCHESTER, SHEFFIELD, WATH

EM1 & EM2

ELECTRIC LOCOMOTIVES

John Hooper

BOOK LAW PUBLICATIONS

ISBN 978-1-909625-19-8

ACKNOWLEDGEMENTS

Over the years of collecting, collating and dissecting the material used to construct this book, a large number of people have willingly given their time to help me produce what is hopefully a worthwhile addition to the vast library of locomotive histories available for historians, enthusiasts and railway modellers alike.

Firstly, I would like to thank David Allen of Book Law Publications for his encouragement and mentoring, and allowing me access to his archive of all things EM1 and EM2. Ian Trivett is another who, over the years, has also encouraged and goaded me into action to get the tome completed in time for '…next years show…'.

David Dunn has supplied numerous images, many of which have found a place in this volume, and I would like to express my gratitude for his time and effort in coming up with the goods every time I asked. Other photographers have willingly sent views of the locomotives of either their own taking or from collections covering a time span of thirty years or more and for that I would like to say thank you to S.Carter, David Christie, Graham Jelly, Eddie Johnson, Ron Hodge, Neville Stead, Brian North, Shaw Plan, The Transport Treasury and the Armstrong Railway Photographic Trust (ARPT).

Staff at the National Archives, Kew, the Search Engine at the National Railway Museum, Manchester Museum of Science & Industry all helped to find those particularly obscure documents required by anyone researching locomotive history.

Stuart Lawton gave me the low-down on the MSW from a Motormans perspective. It was quite enlightening and forthright and entertaining. Thanks Stuart.

Purely by chance I came across a website which was to provide me with something of a missing link between the conception and ending of the 76s – the scrap yard scenes. For coming up trumps in that department, I would like to give thanks to Hugh Searle who not only provided me with said scrapyard views of his own taking, but for also furnishing the images he captured of the run-down of Reddish depot and the dramatic demise of the 76s. Thanks also for reading through the numerous captions I generated.

Finally the Nottingham Model Railway Society have for decades built, run and researched the locomotives and infrastructure of the MSW line. Like most modellers they are continually aiming for perfection and it was through their good offices and Hayden Reed in particular, that I was able to present a suitable and not completely unhappy ending to this tome.

If I have failed to mention anyone with whom I had contact regarding this book, then please forgive me but thanks anyway.

Thank you everyone.

First published in the United Kingdom by
BOOK LAW PUBLICATIONS 2014
382 Carlton Hill, Nottingham, NG4 1JA
Printed and bound by The Amadeus Press, Cleckheaton, West Yorkshire.

CONTENTS

The construction of Wath depot is described elsewhere in this book but this picture illustrates nicely the lightweight construction materials used in order to achieve the desired structure. 26027 stables outside the northern end of the shed, circa 1955. The MSW electrified line is now up and running its future loking bright. Perhaps if the line had been extended coast-to-coast, or down the GC to London, things might have been different. We shall never know. ***Authors coll.***

Full circle! Less than thirty years were to elapse from opening the MSW scheme to its to closure. Class 76 (EM1) 76057 being cannibalised at Reddish. Pantographs gone, internal equipment about to go, and those traction motors on the floor may well have been given up by 76057 too. It is 2nd July 1978 and Crewe has basically handed over the upkeep and maintenance of the remaining members of Class 76 to Reddish. The means of carrying out the work were in place with both jacks and overhead cranes at the ready. The work force was more than familiar with their charges and although spares were not plentiful, they were nearby and available! Three years from now and it would all be done with. No more swapping, changing, taking off one and putting on another. Near miracles would be performed by the personnel at the sharp end as BR washed its hands of the MSW line and all it entailed. ***Hugh P.Searle.***

INTRODUCTION

This historical review of one of the most iconic 'modern' locomotive types had its origins in an east Manchester suburb round about the period when the Manchester, Sheffield & Wath electrification was completed. To a six-year old just becoming aware of the fascination of railways in general, and the local railways in particular, courtesy of an older brother and his friends who roamed the area to the east of our home where there was open ground, reservoirs, bridges and railway lines. One place we often passed during our travels (we regularly covered three miles a day just walking, even taking into account the loitering en route) was Reddish electric depot which had a weird fascination to me because it was home to some very quiet, non-smoking and slow-moving locomotives which were more like the engines on my brother's Hornby-Dublo set. All of the railway locomotives I had encountered thus far had been of the smoke-belching, noisy, and frankly, quite frightening types which in some cases went very fast although most seemed to be lumbering and labouring towards us getting noisier, larger and more intimidating as they did so. Yes we did play on railway embankments and occasionally crossed the tracks but purely as a short-cut. The locomotives at Reddish were nothing like their steam counterparts and so was aroused an unhealthy 'affair' which waxed and waned over the years but was always there in my heart. As I became more aware of the Bo+Bos and Co-Cos, the more fascinated I became. Where did they go when they left the shed? It was always to the north because the wires stopped at Reddish ('...that was the only problem with the MSW, the wires stopped too soon!' as one former Driver put it). A chance trip to Guide Bridge, in a friend's parent's car allowed me and my friend to go onto the station platform and watch the trains for a few minutes. Low and behold there were my electric friends going about their business hauling goods trains and passenger services to, goodness knows where. I had to find out more.

Visits inside the depot at Reddish were basically forbidden to scruffy little urchins like ourselves so roaming the perimeter was to only way of seeing what was happening inside the shed. I noticed that each locomotive had a different number and so every time I went past the depot I looked if anything had changed and of course they had; the numbers I saw last time were different from these numbers! How many of these things were there? The chronology of my indoctrination into trainspotting is somewhat obscure but I remember somebody bringing an Ian Allan ABC, London Midland Region as it turned out, to school whereupon I scanned every page looking for my electric friends. Lo and behold, they were not in there! Mystery time. How many of these books existed and which one held the listing of the Reddish electrics? Enter the Combined volume courtesy of a kindly old Aunt and dear old Christmas. It was thick that combine but towards the back was what I was looking for. There were 58 in one class and 7 in another, and one even had a name just like another friend. It might have been Christmas Day and there was snow on the ground but I wanted to get over to Reddish to 'spot' those electrics'. Parents were consulted, negotiated with and finally convinced that I would be okay as long as I wrapped-up and put my balaclava on. So, off I went on what seemed like a trek, on my own for the first – but not the last – time. I logged the numbers in pencil inside an old notebook and took them home to check, and then underline the 'booty' of my first serious 'spot'. Thereafter it became easy to collect all of the EM1 and EM2 classes such was their frequency of visits to Reddish. I even managed to get into the depot, after asking politely, and was given a conducted tour. Wow, they were big engines. Next came the change in livery followed by names being bestowed on certain ones. It was a few years before I realised that those with train heating boilers got the names.

What about TOMMY; which appeared different from the others and had a smaller cab. But what did that name signify along with that legend beneath? Things to find out, things to do!

Of course train spotting was now part and parcel of my young life and I wanted to travel further afield. There was only so far you could get to in a day on a bicycle. So, to raise the kind of funds required to roam the country I started doing a paper round morning and night. Mrs B, the newsagent I worked for allowed me to have the occasional Saturday off so that I could travel to such places as Crewe, Doncaster, Darlington, Derby, and Sheffield, the latter place via the Woodhead route.

Growing up, periods out of the country, travelling all over the country by train, and generally being an adult with responsibilities meant that railways took a back seat in my life but I still watched the passing scene and took notice of the changes. With curiosity rearing its head, I started purchasing the odd periodical to catch up on what was happening on BR. And there they were, my old friends from Reddish still going and hauling MGR coal trains. Where were the EM2s? Scrapped? No they had all gone abroad apparently bought for a song by the Dutch. However, the Woodhead route was under threat of closure and the 1500V d.c. locomotives that worked the line were to be scrapped. Rumours abounded that the Woodhead route was to be saved and converted to 25kV a.c. but even so the 76s were still doomed. And so this book is a result of that re-kindled curiosity and fascination with the Woodhead electrics.

As an aside, but still part of the story of these locomotives, I list the actual costs of the engines according to the History Cards: 26000 - £18,793; 26001 to 26019, and 26021 to 26044 - £29,278 each; 26020 - £32,138; 26045 - £29,277; 26046 to 26055 - £32,138 each; 26056 and 26057 - £32,139 each. 27000 to 27003 - £63,513 each; 27004 to 27006 - £63,512 each. Fascinating stuff. Enjoy the book.

John Hooper, France 2014.

No.6701 as turned out by the paint shop at Doncaster in February 1941. On 16th January 1939 an order was signed to build seventy of these locomotives at Doncaster, with electrical equipment supplied by Metropolitan Vickers. On 2nd November 1939, with world political events deteriorating and Britain already at war, the order was cut to just one example, the production batch being shelved for the duration of the conflict – until 1950 as it transpired, long after the demise of the LNER. After completion at Doncaster, No.6701's first appearance was at York's old station on 19th February 1941. The event was arranged so that Gresley could show off the prototype to the LNER directors, management officials and the press. Having officially been taken into stock on Saturday 20th September 1941, its first trials took place during the three days Monday 22nd to Wednesday 24th September 1941, on the electrified line between Altrincham and Manchester (London Road) when passenger stock was hauled between the two places. Note that single sandboxes (all lined out) have been fixed not only at each corner of each bogie but twin boxes have been fitted in the centre too. The flexible hoses on the front supplied air, vacuum and steam heating. After these tests with passenger rolling stock, No.6701 was taken back to Doncaster works for storage. However, two weeks later, on Sunday 5th October 1941 No.6701 hauled 45 loaded wagons and two brake vans over the same route. Regenerative brake tests were carried out against the pull of two J39 steam locomotives. The tests continued until 14th October when the prototype was again returned to Doncaster and further storage. *LNER*.

On 18th June 1946, as part of the LNER renumbering scheme, the Bo+Bo became No.6000. With post-war recovery taking time, and knowing that it would be some years before the MSW electrification project was completed, the LNER decided to loan the prototype to the Netherlands State Railways in order to gain some operating experience on the type. This is the EM1 inside the paint shop at Doncaster where it had been safely tucked-away for the duration of the conflict. *W.H.Whitworth*.

(*opposite*) No.6000 departing from Doncaster on the afternoon of Saturday 30th August 1947; the Bo+Bo was now on its way to Harwich and extended loan to the Dutch railways. Arriving at Parkeston Quay during the early hours of Sunday morning, the EM1 was loaded aboard *Essex Ferry* during the following Monday afternoon, ready for a midnight sailing to Zeebrugge. After haulage through Belgium, No.6000 crossed the frontier into Holland and after a couple of weeks of preparations, began running on 15th September 1947. During its time abroad the Bo+Bo worked some 335,000 miles before eventually returning to the United Kingdom on 30th March 1952 for overhaul, and a repaint into British Railways mixed traffic colours. It afterwards took up residency at Ilford e.m.u. depot. Note the major external change made prior to its overseas venture – the large central sandboxes had been removed from each bogie. *Authors coll.*

CHRONOLOGY, FACTS & TRIVIA

1936:

13th November: The *Railway Gazette* published the intention of the LNER to electrify the route between Manchester and Sheffield via Woodhead using the 1500v d.c. overhead system.

1937:

Tenders invited for the supply of seventy sets of electrical equipment for 70 mixed-traffic locomotives.

1939:

January: Seventy locomotives were ordered to be built at Doncaster under seven separate Engine Orders, Nos.348 to 354, of ten engines each.

November: The order was reduced to just one locomotive following the outbreak of WW2 and the postponement of the electrification of the MSW route.

1940:

A start was made on the building of No.6701. The design incorporated two four-wheel bogies which were linked together. Buffers and drawgear were attached to the bogies so that all traction and braking forces were directed through the bogies themselves and not the locomotive body.

August: No.6701 was completed. Testing of the locomotive's running and springing arrangement was conducted on the East Coast Main Line between Doncaster and Retford using a steam locomotive for haulage at speeds up to 60 m.p.h.. Numerous modifications were duly made to the suspension because it was found on some of the early runs that at 20 m.p.h. the locomotive oscillated considerably making riding conditions in the cabs rather uncomfortable. Tests and rectification to the springing were carried on into 1941 until a proper balance was achieved.

1941:

11th February: Painted in apple green livery, No.6701 was shown to the press at York.

September: Classified 0-4+4-0, No.6701 was added to LNER Stock. With the running trials satisfactory, No.6701 was sent to run trials on the Manchester South Junction & Altrincham line (which had been electrified since 1931). After trials and modifications were completed on 14th October, No.6701 was then stored at Doncaster works for the duration of the war.

1945:

September: Reclassified EM1, No.6701 was taken to King's Cross station for official inspection.

21st December: No.6701 was one of the exhibits at the Sheffield Centenary Exhibition.

1946:

June: No.6701 renumbered No.6000.

1947:

August: No.6000 was taken back to the MSJ&A line after running further high speed tests (up to 70 m.p.h.) on the ECML. Back at Doncaster it was spruced-up for its Continental adventure before being hauled to Harwich on the 30th.

1st September: No.6000 was taken aboard the *ESSEX FERRY* at Harwich for the sea crossing to Zeebrugge and the start of its stint of working over the railways of Holland.

15th September: No.6000 had its first run under power in Holland.

1948:

No.6000 was proving its worth in Holland and during its first six weeks of service it had run 2,000 miles each week on passenger trains loaded to 330 tons. Goods trains of 1,600 tons were handled easily by the Bo+Bo with impressive acceleration figures. By early 1948, with some 18,000 miles running under its belt, No.6000 started to develop some serious running problems concerning the bogie springing, body springing, and the articulated linkage between the bogies. However, a solution was eventually found after some radical changes to all three springing arrangements during March. The changes worked and although wear and tear was heavy on the bogie linkage (and would remain so throughout the lifetime of the class), No.6000 was a proven success and the necessary modifications were made to the drawings of the production batch.

1950:

April: 26001 and 26002 were taken from Gorton to Dukinfield for the installation of electrical components. Meanwhile four more frames have been laid at Gorton works.

May: Work on the erection of a new depot, for the MSW electric locomotives, has begun at Wath. *See* later for a description of how the civil engineers tackled the problem of mining subsidence which was rife throughout the whole area.

May: A Y3 Sentinel locomotive (8169) arrived at Dinting in connection with the MSW electrification work.

August: The first ten electric locomotives have been erected at Gorton and sent to Dukinfield for electric component fittings. Nos.11 to 14 have now been laid down at Gorton.

18th October: 26001, the first EM1 to be completed, was towed to Woodhead and back to test its bearings. The locomotive was due to travel south to Ilford for trials on the newly electrified line between Shenfield and Liverpool Street.

3rd November – Friday: Nos.26001 and 26002 began trials, including current collection tests, regeneration and air brake tests on the electrified section of railway between Ilford and Shenfield. Firstly with 26001 and 26002 were coupled together but ran light. Later brake vans were coupled between the locomotives, then with both passenger and goods vehicles. On Sunday 5th November No.26002 was photographed at Chadwell Heath with a nine-coach test train. There was never any intention to use these locomotives on the local services and testing was only being carried out there because no overhead line had been completed on the MSW scheme. The regenerative braking feature on these locomotives also had to be tested thoroughly and Brentwood bank was considered ideal for the purpose.

12th November: A visit to Gorton works on this date revealed 26003 and 26004 in the Paint shop whilst 26016, 26017 and 26018 were under construction in the erecting shop.

1951:

General: In 1951 it was estimated that each of the new Co-Co EM2 electric locomotives for the MSW electrification was going to cost £37,400. This compared with £16,000 for a new Class 5 4-6-0, £78,200 for a 1,600 h.p. Co-Co diesel-electric locomotive, and £138,700 for a 2,500 h.p. gas-turbine-electric locomotive. *See* elsewhere for actual costs, according to the Engine History Cards.

June: Shortly after completion, No.26014 attended an exhibition of Rolling Stock in the original passenger station yard at York. No.26020 went one better and was exhibited at the showcase Festival of Britain on the South Bank site in London. Its attendance at that particular venue, from February to September, and then its use to haul the first train through the new Woodhead tunnel (*see* later) ensured that the would EM1 gain immortality and the Bo+Bo is now part of the National Collection wearing the 1951 black lined livery – not to mention the stainless steel handrails it was built with for the 1951 *FofB* exhibition.
The first members of the batch of ten – 26001 to 26010 – sent to the GE lines were returned to the MSW line as the current was switched on in the Wath area. Crew training at Wath was now begun in earnest.

Wath locomotive depot – Because of coal mining subsidence being a fact of life in the area, and settlement of the ground where the shed was being erected expected to sink about 5ft, a novel method of ensuring minimal damage to the new shed was employed from the outset. Independent engine pits, hinged in short lengths throughout, with the shed designed in a series of braced portal frames, with two anchor frames at each end. Intermediate frames were in pairs, double hinged at each foot and connected to the next pair with side rails in which slotted joints were provided. This enabled the building to settle without serious distortion. Although not as severe as expected, settlement did reach 3ft at the eastern end of the shed and about 2ft 9ins. at the other end by the time the ground movement had ceased. No distortion of the structure had taken place and only the slotted holes in the side rails showed that any movement had occurred, whilst sections of the concrete slab floor did require taking up and relaying. The track was also affected with coach screws pulled out of the chairs and some chairs actually broken.

1952:

General:
Testing became necessary throughout the year after adhesion problems brought some 850 ton coal trains to a halt (even with banking assistance) on the inclines of the Worsborough branch. Connected to those problems were bogie centre pin distortions and fractures. Once again the value of tests under actual working conditions proved their worth and changes were made not only to components, but also to driving practices. Nos.26030 and 26034, which had been suitably modified were used for the extensive testing period.

31st January: Hauled by No.26026, a trial train consisting four passenger vehicles was run between Wath yard and Penistone (was this the Press run mentioned elsewhere).

4th February: The first stage of the MSW scheme, some 18 miles and 78 chains, was inaugurated between Wath and Dunford Bridge. Electric working of freight trains commenced between Wath yard and Penistone. This particular event saw the completion of Phase One of the MSW electrification. Westbound trains continued their journey with steam motive power.

28th March: No.6000 returned to the United Kingdom from Holland, and was then renumbered 26000 at Stratford.

30th June: 26000 was named TOMMY during an official ceremony at Liverpool Street station in London. During the period that it was working in Holland, No.26000 ran more than 325,000 miles in passenger and freight service.

1953:

19th & 20th September: No.26020 was exhibited at Doncaster Locomotive Works which was celebrating its Centenary.

2nd November: From this date all goods trains between Dewsnap sidings and Woodhead were electrically hauled.2nd November: From this date all goods trains between Dewsnap sidings and Woodhead were electrically hauled.

1954:

General: The year of full opening of the Woodhead tunnel, and near completion of the MSW electrification project.

4th May: The first electric locomotive to enter Reddish depot was a rather grubby looking 26040. Although incomplete, the depot was not far from being ready to accept the EM1 class for maintenance.

18th May to 10th June: Shortly after completion, EM2 No.27002 went on exhibition at the International Railway Congress held at Willesden roundhouse until 4th June.

30th May: EM1 Nos.26001 (leading) and 26016 were the first electric locomotives to traverse the new Woodhead tunnel. With all four cabs packed with railway officials and contractors representatives, the two Bo+Bos made the sedate eastbound (Up) passage of the bore under their own power. No.26001 had No.1 end leading whilst No.26016 had No.2 end leading.

3rd June: EM1 No.26020 hauled the first train through the new Woodhead tunnel and was suitably fitted with stainless steel handrails for the Up journey from Woodhead to Dunford Bridge. No.26020 was certainly building up its celebrity points.

14th June: Full electric working between Manchester and Penistone commenced.

1st August: Reddish depot was visited and the following locomotives were on shed: EM1 26003, 26016, 26017, 26020, 26021, 26022, 26025, 26031, 26040, 26050, 26051, 26052, 26054, 26055, 26056, 26057. EM2 27000, 27001, 27002, 27003. Besides these, another ten EM1s were stabled at Guide Bridge alongside the Stalybridge line.

14th September: Tuesday – Immaculately turned-out EM2 No.27000 arrived at Manchester (London Road) station with the first through electrically hauled passenger working over the Woodhead route from Sheffield (Victoria). The train was in fact a one-off special conveying railway officials, guests and civic dignitaries. Full ordinary passenger services did not start until the following Monday 20th September.

1955:

General: During the year train heating boilers were fitted to EM1s Nos.26020, 26046, 26047, 26048 and 26049 at Dukinfield Works.

3rd January: As one of the final elements in the MSW electrification scheme, and to give greater flexibility around the Sheffield area, the section of line between Darnall and Rotherwood was electrified.

1956:

1st September: EM2 No.27000, painted green, lined out (black and orange), with black frames and silver bogies (the first MSW electric locomotive in this livery), was used on a special working for the British Association, from Sheffield (Victoria) to Reddish depot, then back to Penistone and on to Wath..

General: By the end of the year olive green lined livery began to be applied to EM1s, No.26025 was the first of the class to be so treated.

1957:

28th January: No.26025 was the first standard green EM1 noted in Sheffield.

The opening ceremony for the new Woodhead tunnel took place on Thursday 3rd June 1954 with 'celebrity' EM1 26020 doing the honours of hauling the special passenger train through the tape and then the tunnel itself. The opening speech, and the driving of the Bo+Bo through the tape, was performed by the Minister of Transport & Civil Aviation, Mr Alan Lennox-Boyd. The Minister can be seen here scaling the steps into the cab of 26020 before taking control of the locomotive. The fact that the said gentleman was some 6ft 7ins. tall would have no doubt made him aware of the restricted clearance through the doorway and into the already crowded cab. The locomotive's highly polished state was a credit to the personnel who got it ready for the occasion but it was no stranger to pomp this particular EM1. First the Festival of Britain, then Doncaster Works Centenary Exhibition, now the Woodhead opening! What next preservation? Surely not! What about TOMMY? *BLPubs.*

26020

(opposite) **Although 26020, with its draped Union flags intertwined with the BR lion & wheel emblem, is supposed to be the Authors chosen subject of this illustration, it is worth examining the host of people milling around the point of ceremony, including those on the hillside on the opposite side of the main line. The special train was already drawn up to the new station platform so that the various dignitaries and invited guests could board the carriages for the journey through the tunnel; full electric working through to Sheffield did not take place until late September. However, before that the Minister had to go through the gambit of the PR exercise for the sake of the press, as here, where smiles and waves were the order of the day; although Lennox-Boyd apparently had something of a happy (public) disposition anyway. There are many people in the photograph who do not know the area and have arrived in suits only, whilst others, who were aware of Woodhead's moody weather, even at the height of summer, have brought suitable inclement weather coats just in case. The film crew on the temporary scaffold platform seem unaware that their perch is secured to one of the catenary masts and that the overhead wire of the Down line is virtually within touching distance perhaps the current for that line was switched out! As the day unfolded and everything returned to normal, Woodhead got back its demeanour of isolation although twenty-odd years of trains coming and going were to shatter the quiet every so often just as it had done for the previous 100-odd years. Now, it is as peaceful as ever except for the busy A628 road above the tunnel mouth. *Book Law Publications*.**

(opposite, bottom) **Completing the dream! 26013 runs into the station precincts at Guide Bridge with a westbound Class C freight after through working via the new Woodhead tunnel began officially on Monday 14th June 1954. *Authors coll.***

1958:

18th June: No.26026 in the company of new diesel and steam locomotives, and rolling stock, was exhibited at Blast Lane goods depot in Sheffield.

1959:

16th January: EM1 No.26018 was exhibited at Lincoln.

1962:

19th September: British Transport Commission announced closure of Gorton locomotive works by mid-1963.

1963:

21st April: As and from this date, with the impending closure of Gorton Works, all EM1 and EM2 overhauls were to be carried out at Crewe Works.

24th April: EM2 No.27001 ARIADNE was the last locomotive repaired at Gorton and was put back into traffic on this date.

31st May: Gorton Works closed.

1964:

27th July: Woodhead passenger station closed.

September: Gorton Works, though closed for some fifteen months, was still intact at this date and minor modifications, concerning train heating boilers, were carried out on a number of EM1s (26000, 26051 + others) by fitters sent from Crewe.

1965:

February: The long term future of the MSW Woodhead route is assured when it was confirmed in a report entitled *Beeching Part Two - Trunk Routes*.

30th May: MSW extension to Tinsley yard opened with the catenary provided to give conversion to AC from DC.

4th October: Sheffield Victoria station lost half its passenger services when a new direct cord line was opened at Nunnery to allow services to be re-routed and to use Midland station instead.

1966:

General: Yellow warning panels were introduced to the ends of the engines.

17th January: It was announced that all passenger services currently using Woodhead route would in future be diverted to use the Hope Valley route.

5th September: Sheffield Victoria loses further services when GC London extension route closed.

October: The first of the EM1s to be dealt with, E26037, was turned out in blue livery.

1967:

January: Withdrawal of the MSW passenger services announced!
3rd August: EM1 No.26014 was towed from Reddish depot to Soho electric depot, Birmingham for conversion to AC/DC by G.E.C. Witton. It went into General Electric Co.'s Soho works. The converted EM1 was to have trials hauling freight on the WCML in place of the AL6 a.c. locomotives which were giving trouble at that time. The conversion/trial was obviously not a success and we hear no more of the aforementioned.

1968:

February: E26046 was seen wearing the new British Rail double-reverse arrow motif.

28th March: EM1 class were designated TOPS Class 76, whilst EM2 became Class 77.

1st June 1968 – 26052 hauled the Guide Bridge–Sheffield Vic.–Guide Bridge section of the Scottish Region *Grand Tour No.5* train, from Edinburgh, on this date.

September: The seven Co-Co Class 77 (EM2) locomotives withdrawn and put into store.

1969:

General: One of the TOMMY nameplates, mounted on a polished wooden plaque was presented to the Nederlands Railway by British Railways. 26000 had lost its two worksplates by 27th August.

1969 cont./

13th August: Withdrawal of the Manchester (Piccadilly)–Sheffield (Victoria) passenger services was approved.

20th August: In conjunction with the sale of the EM2 class to Holland, 27002 hauled a special passenger (demonstration) train from Reddish depot depart 1100 to Sheffield (Victoria) arrive 1218. A speed limit of 75 m.p.h. was authorised over the otherwise 65 m.p.h. restricted route.

22nd September: EM2s Nos.27000, 27001, 27003, 27005, 27006 were hauled from Bury to Harwich for shipment to Holland.

23rd September: Nos.27002 and 27004 followed the other five from Reddish. The locomotives cost the Dutch Railways approximately £5,000 each and they were to be converted to right-hand drive in Holland.

1970:

General: This was to be the last year of passenger train haulage by the MSW electric locomotives over the Woodhead line.

January: Merry-Go-Round coal trains, originating from pits in South Yorkshire and bound for Fiddlers Ferry power station, started running via the Woodhead line this month. Double-headed MU-fitted class 76s hauled the trains between Rotherwood and Mottram yards.

3rd January: Saturday – a fateful day for the MSW route as the last electrically hauled passenger services were run.

March: The first withdrawals from class EM1 took place when three engines: 26000, 26005, 26017, 26035, and 26042 were all condemned.

16th April: The first of a series of tests of MGR coal train working from Wath yard over the Worsborough branch were conducted.

19th April: Ex-works E26013, complete with newly fitted multiple units cables, visited the Crewe Electric Depot Open Day.

October: MGR coal trains, up to 1,550 tons in weight, started regular running between Wath yard and Mottram with two multiple unit fitted Class 76 on the front and two multiple unit 76s banking from Wentworth Junction to Penistone where the trains stopped to detach the banking engines. From 1972 the banking engines detached at West Silkstone junction.

1973:

General: During this year all repairs to Class 76 were undertaken at Doncaster Works.

1974:

General: The final Diagrams issued for the EM1s as Class 76 in 1974 were as follows:

76-aV Basic locomotive with no heating boiler but with vacuum brake.
76-bX Dual braked.
76-cV Basic locomotive with heating boiler, and vacuum brake.
76-dA Air brake modification.

The lower case suffix shows the separate variety whilst the upper case suffix shows the brake type.

General: Crewe resumed repair of the class in January 1974 after the part closure of Swindon shops and a reshuffle of the workload whereby Doncaster took on some of the locomotive types formerly dealt with at Swindon and handed back the Class 76 to Crewe maintenance; although Doncaster again took on the class in 1975, albeit in conjunction with Crewe, to alleviate a shortage of motive power on the MSW line.

22nd September: 76054 took part in an exhibition at Barrow Hill roundhouse.

1976:

General: An ER/LMR joint committee was established to consider the future of the MSW Woodhead route.

November: 76050, which became the first EM1 to be renumbered in the TOPS classification, was renumbered 76038.

1978:

General: By January Class 76 overhauls and repairs at Crewe works appear to have ceased; 76039 was the last recorded repair at CW (December 1977). All repairs from hereon were carried out at Reddish but, *see* below!

26th April 1978, Penistone – A pair of 76's (numbers unknown) were derailed at Huddersfield Jct. whilst working an MGR train.

September: It was reported that 76024 went to CW for repair during this month.

27th October: 76011+76025 hauled the HRT *Trans Pennine Freighter* railtour from Manchester Piccadilly.

2nd December: 76030 piloted 40106 from Guide Bridge to Rotherwood with the Wirral Railway Circle *North Country Continental*.

15th September: 76016+76007 hauled the MNLPS *Strongbow Express* railtour.

1979:

2nd December: Worsborough branch – Despite the proposed closure of this line, continuous welded rail was being laid on concrete sleepers whilst the overhead wires and supportive catenary underwent considerable maintenance also!

1980:

10th January: Unusually, a Class 76 visited Manchester Piccadilly station when, at 0500 on this day, 76051 was sent to pick up a guard who was required at Reddish depot! The circumstances behind this event had started the night before when the electric multiple unit working the 2300 to Hadfield caught fire in the station and a diesel multiple unit from Longsight was substituted.

15th June: Tinsley – 76033 was amongst the many locomotives which took part in the depot Open Day held to coincide with the centenary celebrations of ASLEF.

17th July: *The Worsborough Banker* railtour - This short and unusually mid-week evening railtour was organised by the RCTS Sheffield branch to tour the still open d.c. electrified lines east of Penistone. Though starting at Midland station, the six-coach train was hauled to Rotherwood sidings by two Class 20 diesel locomotives (20066 and 20095) which then handed over to 76003 for the leg to Penistone where 76001 coupled onto the rear of the train which departed at 1941 for Wath yard. 76001 then ran round its train for the return leg to Penistone with the ascent of Worsborough bank en route. It was noted – cynically by some – that recent relaying of ballast and continuous welded rail had taken place on the incline. Back at Penistone, reached at three minutes past nine, 76003 was waiting to relieve 76001. Back to Sheffield but taking the line from Woodburn Jct to Tinsley yard where the Bo+Bo ran round its train for the journey back to Rotherwood but this time using the north to east connection at Woodburn Jct. The same 20's which hauled the tour from the former Midland station did the honours in reverse and the participants detrained at Sheffield at 2253.

7th October - Closure of the MSW route is announced and will come into effect on 1st June 1981!

1981:

18th July : MSW 'Woodhead' Route – Closed. Last train was 6M62 the Parkeston Quay–Liverpool Edge Hill Speedlink hauled by 76006 and 76014 which apparently passed through Woodhead at 0508 hrs that morning. 0600 hours saw the final shift of men sign off – the MSW route was no more!

To prevent wholesale theft (by no means a modern phenomenon), the overhead wiring was taken down almost immediately after the closure of the line and was certainly completed before the end of 1981.

76039 (ex26048 HECTOR) had a cab removed to provide an exhibit at the Manchester Museum of Science & Industry.

1982:

Track lifting of the Worsborough bank section of the MSW route between Penistone and Wath was carried out.

1983:

Track lifting between Hadfield and Deepcar/Stocksbridge began in 1983. The rest of the existing route was required for ongoing local services and access to industrial premises.

14th May: Reddish depot closed and the resident 76s still languishing about the place were taken to either Guide Bridge or Ashburys to await buyers from the scrap metal industry.

1984:

Week ending 25th February: Last of the Class 76s sold for scrap were cut up. Except for 26020, the No.1 end cab off 76039, and a few odd bits of locomotives salvaged by enthusiasts, the MSW Class EM1 ceased to exist. Of the seven EM2s, no less than three remain intact and preserved!

The section of the line from Hadfield to Manchester's Piccadilly station was converted to 25kV ac so that the Class 506 emus also ended their working days during the decade.

(below) **Reddish, Friday 17th July 1981. This was the last full day of working on the MSW line but most of the locomotives here were not taking part in the operations that day. Nearest to the camera is 76029 which, like the others on show, was looking rather smart but much of the sheen to the paintwork was due to heavy rain which, in typical English summertime fashion had lashed down at various times of the day, especially over the western side of Woodhead. However, it was not a celebration, parade or carnival on that seventeenth day of July 1981 but an abrupt end of what was Britain's first main line electrification scheme. One which proved to all and sundry that electric traction was the future means of motive power for BR if the country was to prosper. Meanwhile, the question of what to do with all that scrap metal was not to be answered for nearly two years as Reddish became the resting place for most of the class. Note the '40' tucked up in the middle of the row; what was in store for that monster? *Hugh P.Searle.***

ALLOCATIONS, DEPOTS & STABLING POINTS: CLASS EM1 & EM2

Once the depot at Reddish was commissioned, all of the EM1s and EM2s were allocated to that place and were never again allocated to any other establishment. However, before June 1954 both classes - including every EM1 and the first three EM2s - spent time at either Gorton, Ilford, or Wath, or at all three depots. Even Darnall and Dinting depots got a 'look-in' pre-Reddish.

26000 Ilford 1/7/52, Gorton 1/3/53, Reddish 19/6/54.
26001 Gorton 27/10/50 (tallowed down), Ilford 1/12/50 (on loan then stored) (returned to traffic 16/3/52), Wath 22/3/52, Gorton 21/3/53, Reddish 19/6/54.
26002 Gorton 27/10/50 (tallowed down), Ilford 1/12/50 (on loan then stored) (returned to traffic 16/3/52), Wath 22/3/52, Gorton 21/3/53, Wath 16/5/53, Gorton 26/12/53, Reddish 19/6/54.
26003 Gorton 15/11/50 (tallowed down), Ilford 1/12/50 (on loan then stored) (returned to traffic 16/3/52), Ilford 22/3/52, Wath 20/7/52, Gorton 21/3/53, Dinting 6/53, Wath 27/3/54, Reddish 19/6/54.
26004 Gorton 14/2/51 (tallowed down) (to traffic 16/3/52), Ilford 22/3/52, Wath 9/52, Gorton 21/3/53, Reddish 19/6/54.
26005 Gorton 25/1/51 (tallowed down) (to traffic 16/3/52), Ilford 22/3/52, Gorton 21/3/53, Dinting 6/53, Wath 27/3/54, Reddish 19/6/54.
26006 Gorton 25/1/51 (tallowed down) (to traffic 16/3/52), Ilford 22/3/52, Wath 28/7/52, Gorton 21/3/53, Reddish 19/6/54.
26007 Gorton 14/2/51 (tallowed down) (to traffic 16/3/52), Ilford 22/3/52, Gorton 21/3/53, Reddish 19/6/54.
26008 Gorton 17/3/51 (tallowed down) (to traffic 16/3/52), Ilford 22/3/52, Gorton 21/3/53, Reddish 19/6/54.
26009 Gorton 17/3/51 (tallowed down) (to traffic 16/3/52), Ilford 22/3/52, Gorton 21/3/53, Reddish 19/6/54.
26010 Gorton 17/3/51 (tallowed down) (to traffic 16/3/52), Ilford 22/3/52, Gorton 21/3/53, Reddish 19/6/54.
26011 Gorton 31/5/51 (tallowed down) (to traffic 16/3/52), Wath 22/3/52, Gorton 21/3/53, Wath 18/4/53, Gorton 24/4/54, Reddish 19/6/54.
26012 Gorton 7/5/51 (tallowed down), to traffic 16/3/52, Wath 22/3/52, Gorton 26/12/53, Reddish 19/6/54.
26013 Gorton 31/5/51 (tallowed down), to traffic 16/3/52, Wath 22/3/52, Gorton 19/7/53, Wath 5/9/53, Gorton 27/3/54, Reddish 19/6/54.
26014 Gorton 27/5/51 (tallowed down), to traffic 16/3/52, Wath 22/3/52, Gorton 21/3/53, Wath 18/4/53, Gorton 27/3/54, Reddish 19/6/54.
26015 Gorton 26/7/51 (tallowed down), to traffic 16/3/52, Wath 22/3/52, Gorton 31/10/53, Wath 26/12/53, Reddish 19/6/54.
26016 Gorton 25/7/51 (tallowed down), to traffic 16/3/52, Wath 22/3/52, Gorton 27/3/54, Reddish 19/6/54.
26017 Gorton 31/7/51 (tallowed down), to traffic 16/3/52, Wath 22/3/52, Gorton 27/3/54, Wath 24/4/54, Reddish 19/6/54.
26018 Gorton 5/9/51 (tallowed down), to traffic 16/3/52, Wath 22/3/52, Gorton 3/53, Wath 16/5/53, Gorton 27/3/54, Reddish 19/6/54.
26019 Gorton 25/9/51 (tallowed down), to traffic 16/3/52, Wath 22/3/52, Gorton 27/3/53, Dinting 6/53, Reddish 19/6/54.
26020 Gorton 17/2/51 (tallowed down), Festival of Britain 21/4/51, to store 6/10/51, to traffic 16/3/52, Wath 22/3/52, Gorton 16/5/53, Darnall 24/4/54, Gorton 22/5/54, Reddish 19/6/54.
26021 Gorton 2/10/51 (tallowed down), to traffic 16/3/52, Wath 22/3/52, Gorton 16/5/53, Wath 5/9/53, Reddish 19/6/54.
26022 Gorton 20/9/51 (tallowed down), to traffic 16/3/52, Wath 22/3/52, Gorton 21/3/53, Dinting 6/53, Reddish 19/6/54.
26023 Gorton 20/9/51 (tallowed down), to traffic 16/3/52, Wath 22/3/52, Gorton 5/9/53, Wath 31/10/53, Reddish 19/6/54.
26024 Gorton 25/9/51 (tallowed down), to traffic 16/3/52, Wath 22/3/52, Gorton 28/11/53, Reddish 19/6/54.
26025 Gorton 4/1/52 (tallowed down), to traffic 16/3/52, Wath 22/3/52, Gorton 27/3/54, Reddish 19/6/54.
26026 Gorton 4/1/52 (tallowed down), to traffic 16/3/52, Wath 22/3/52, Gorton 23/1/54, Reddish 19/6/54.
26027 Gorton 24/1/52 (tallowed down), to traffic 16/3/52, Wath 22/3/52, Gorton 24/4/54, Reddish 19/6/54.
26028 Gorton 16/1/52 (tallowed down), to traffic 16/3/52, Wath 22/3/52, Gorton 24/4/54, Reddish 19/6/54.
26029 Gorton 28/12/51 (tallowed down), to traffic 16/3/52, Wath 22/3/52, Gorton 19/7/53, Reddish 19/6/54.
26030 Gorton 28/12/51 (tallowed down), to traffic 16/3/52, Wath 22/3/52, Gorton 21/3/53, Wath 19/7/53, Reddish 19/6/54.
26031 Gorton 11/1/52 (tallowed down), to traffic 16/3/52, Wath 22/3/52, Gorton 11/7/53, Wath 28/11/53, Reddish 19/6/54.
26032 Gorton 16/1/52 (tallowed down), to traffic 16/3/52, Wath 22/3/52, Gorton 11/7/53, Wath 31/10/53, Reddish 19/6/54.
26033 Gorton 18/1/52 (tallowed down), to traffic 16/3/52, Wath 22/3/52, Gorton 26/12/53, Reddish 19/6/54.
26034 Gorton 18/1/52 (tallowed down), to traffic 16/3/52, Wath 22/3/52, Gorton 21/3/53, Wath 11/7/53, Reddish 19/6/54.
26035 Gorton 24/1/52 (tallowed down), to traffic 16/3/52, Wath 22/3/52, Gorton 18/4/53, Wath 19/7/53, Gorton 22/5/54, Reddish 19/6/54.
26036 Gorton 1/2/52 (tallowed down), to traffic 16/3/52, Wath 22/3/52, Gorton 28/11/53, Reddish 19/6/54.
26037 Gorton 1/2/52 (tallowed down), to traffic 16/3/52, Wath 22/3/52, Gorton 23/1/54, Wath 27/3/54, Reddish 19/6/54.
26038 Wath 4/4/52, Gorton 27/3/54, Reddish 19/6/54.
26039 Wath 12/4/52, Gorton 26/12/53, Reddish 19/6/54.
26040 Wath 21/4/52, Gorton 31/10/53, Reddish 19/6/54.
26041 Wath 21/4/52, Gorton 31/10/53, Reddish 19/6/54.
26042 Wath 19/5/52, Gorton 21/3/53, Wath 27/3/54, Reddish 19/6/54.
26043 Wath 29/5/52, Gorton 21/3/53, Wath 27/3/54, Reddish 19/6/54.
26044 Wath 11/6/52, Gorton 21/3/53, Wath 26/12/53, Reddish 19/6/54.
26045 Wath 26/6/52, Gorton 21/3/53, Wath 28/11/53, Reddish 19/6/54.

26046 Wath 8/8/52, Gorton 21/3/53, Wath 26/12/53, Reddish 19/6/54.
26047 Wath 22/8/52, Gorton 21/3/53, Wath 26/12/53, Reddish 19/6/54.
26048 Wath 10/9/52, Gorton 21/3/53, Wath 23/1/54, Reddish 19/6/54.
26049 Wath 27/9/52, Gorton 21/3/53, Wath 23/1/54, Reddish 19/6/54.
26050 Wath 19/11/52, Gorton Works 19/11/52 (stored), Gorton 21/3/53, Wath 6/2/54, Reddish 19/6/54.
26051 Wath 18/12/52, Gorton Works 18/12/52 (stored), Gorton 21/3/53, Wath 24/2/54, Reddish 19/6/54.
26052 Gorton 31/1/53 (stored), Wath 13/3/54, Reddish 19/6/54.
26053 Gorton 11/3/53 (stored), Wath 20/3/54, Reddish 19/6/54.
26054 Gorton 23/4/53, Reddish 19/6/54.
26055 Gorton 6/6/53, Reddish 19/6/54.
26056 Gorton 19/7/53, Reddish 19/6/54.
26057 Gorton 26/8/53, Reddish 19/6/54.

27000 Wath 28/12/53, Reddish 19/6/54.
27001 Wath 22/3/54, Reddish 19/6/54.
27002 Wath 18/5/54, Reddish 19/6/54.
27003 Reddish 5/8/54.
27004 Reddish 18/9/54.
27005 Reddish 11/12/54.
27006 Reddish 31/12/54.

As an aside, an interesting point was made in the August 1975 issue of the *Railway Observer* concerning the display of depot codes on locomotives at that period. In the five years from July 1970 (when a small rectangular transfer was adopted in favour of the previous cast metal oval shedplate - 9C) to July 1975 no less than five different, but nonetheless similar, styles of transfer had been applied to indicate the home depot of locomotives. The transfer was usually located beneath the locomotive number and the changes which occurred were as follows:
1. July 1970 - The depot name in full with the old series shed code below - REDDISH / 9C.
2. October 1971 - The depot name only, omitting the old shed code - REDDISH.
3. February 1973 - The depot name with abbreviation below - REDDISH / RS.
4. February 1974 - The depot abbreviation only - RS.
5. July 1975 - A reversion to the third, February 1973 style, but with the depot name set in italics - *REDDISH* / RS.

Of course not all of the Class 76 carried all of the above changes, and it would be unusual if any three of the five examples was ever carried by any one locomotive. More to the point, did Reddish depot ever change any of the transfers once applied? Both Crewe and Doncaster works were involved with maintaining the class during the period in question so it was highly probable that a number, if not all of these examples were carried by the class. However, photographic evident has shown that hardly any of the MSW locomotives carried any of the above shed codes, metal or transfer!

In the shadow of the servicing shed at Darnall motive power depot on Sunday 26th August 1956, 26023 is the 'filler' in a sandwich of EM1s with 26024 to the west and 26046 at the east. Note that all the pantographs are lowered, signifying a lengthy period out-of-use (36 hours or so) before going back into service. *F.W.Hampson (ARPT).*

The lightweight cladding covering the steel skeleton of Wath shed is testament to the cautious approach in building an engine shed in this notoriously subsidence affected mining area. However, a depot was required and its construction solutions are described elsewhere. On a somewhat sunny afternoon, 26002 peeps out of the north end of the shed where 7 and 35-day checks were carried out on the EM1s by the maintenance staff. *N.E.Stead coll.*

The classic view of Wath depot from the road bridge located at the south end of the site. It is 29th October 1961 – Sunday of course – and enthusiasts seemingly make their own ways around the place. More than fifteen EM1s are on shed but we only have the line-up nearest the camera recorded: 26046, 26014, 26051, and 26056, the latter supporting the rumour that the namers also worked for a living. Note the lack of diesels with not even a shunting type in sight. *Transport Treasury.*

April showers! Wath as seen from the same roadway on Saturday 25th April 1981. The depot's layout hadn't changed much over the twenty years since the previous illustration was recorded but the motive power had certainly gone through a transition. Barely five of the MSW locomotives are stabled on this date whilst diesels have virtually taken over. Another few months and the electrics will have gone for good. Like a 'domino effect' the depot too would cease to have a reason for existence as the coalfield which it had served so loyally came to the end of its life. *S.Carter*.

Penistone SP. Nos.26025 and 26044 are seen stabled on a stub siding – the temporary stabling point – on the Down side of Penistone station, at the western end of the platforms on 26th June 1954. *J.W.Armstrong (ARPT)*.

(above) **Rotherwood stabling point, 21st April 1981. All of the locomotives in view are MU equipped and have their pantographs raised, ready for the next westbound job. Time, however, was running out.** ***Hugh P.Searle.*** *(below)* **Long before a stabling point was established on the south (Down) side of the main line at Guide Bridge, the EM1s were usually stabled at weekends on the sidings alongside the branch to Stalybridge – which veered northwards just east of the station. However, singleton locomotives sometimes took advantage of this short stub siding located between the platform ends and the goods shed. No.26027 has bagged the spot on this undated weekend whilst in the distance its sisters hide behind rolling stock on the aforementioned sidings.** ***Transport Treasury.***

A temporary stabling point was established at Dunford yard – prior to the opening of the new Woodhead tunnel – where exchange from steam to electric motive power and vice-versa was performed. The location was actually in use for just over two years although there was no weekend 'loitering' during that time. Engines ran light to Wath in the absence of a 'working' trip after freight traffic ceased on Saturday afternoons. This is 26025 waiting for the next eastbound freight to emerge from the old tunnel. ***Transport Treasury.***

26027 shares the electric locomotive servicing shed at Darnall with 26036 on 27th August 1955. This short-lived electric locomotive facility had been erected at Darnall for this class. Note that the overhead wire runs through the shed; although there was a switch to cut off the current when the need arose. Consisting of two roads, with provision for expansion, the building was located at the north-west corner of the steam locomotive shed site alongside the main-line. Ever wonder where all those route indicating discs came from? Take a look on the right by the wall. ***Transport Treasury.***

Reddish depot Tuesday 4th May 1954 with 26040 testing the catenary layout before building work was completed and the depot commissioned in the summer. This was the first electric locomotive to venture onto the Reddish site and so this picture has some historical significance even though the Bo+Bo is in a somewhat deplorable external condition. ***Brian Green.***

Reddish depot viewed from the elevation of Sandfold Lane on Tuesday 2nd August 1977. This vista of the depot shows the south face of the building with the admin./workshop section on the extreme left, the lofty repair shop centre, and the two road servicing shed forming the east side. The storage roads immediately east of that shop accommodated the three-car Manchester-Glossop-Hadfield units when they were not in service. Further storage roads were added piecemeal over the years since the depot was opened in 1954. On the extreme right of the illustration is the main line from Manchester (Central) and Trafford Park to Guide Bridge, known as the Fallowfield Loop. The land area on which the depot was built once contained a couple of reservoirs which were filled-in to enable BR to erect the building. The amount of land between the depot and the main line appears big enough to erect another similar sized building or at least another four to six servicing roads; whether or not expansion of the place was in the minds of those who planned and authorised Reddish depot at the beginning is unknown but by the time the place was up and running, 1500V d.c. electric traction had already been passed over for the more efficient 25 kV which had been proven as 'the future' by the French railways. Reddish did not always have such a variety of motive power on display. The early days consisted of EM1, EM2, and the Glossop units only but diesel multiple units crept in, followed by various diesel locomotives on occasion. Of the diesels, perhaps the most famous of them were the two six-car Midland Pullman units which were serviced and stabled here from 1960 to 1966, during their time working the Manchester (Central)–London (St Pancras) service via the old Midland route. On view today are 76041, 40027, an unidentified Class 47 and 24022; about normal for 1977. 'Celebrity' 76020, waiting to depart for Doncaster and a life in preservation, was in the formation of rolling stock on the right hand track where 24022 was stabled. When BR eventually vacated the site, the depot building became the target for vandalism and this former 'jewel-in-the-crown' maintenance depot became nothing more than a damaged and derelict shell waiting to be demolished. ***Hugh P.Searle.***

The northern aspect of Reddish depot in May 1983 when the majority of the class had departed for 'pastures anew' in South Yorkshire. *Hugh P.Searle.* *(below)* **A virtually empty repair and lifting shop at Reddish in June 1983. This is the view looking to the north with lots of redundant equipment and spare parts lying around the place. The solitary occupant appears to be a passenger carrying vehicle located on the underfloor re-profiling wheel lathe. Even with its oil soaked floors and pits, the shop still looked bright and airy. When Reddish was decommissioned, a large number of components off the wheel lathe were relocated to a similar appliance at High Meads diesel shops in Stratford. It would be interesting to know where the Matterson jacks ended up. *Hugh P.Searle.***

Reddish Depot maintenance log - Tuesday 12th and Wednesday 13th March 1963

A remarkable and highly detailed document lodged in the archive of the NRM consists many thousands of pages of information as to the day-to-day running (hour by hour would perhaps be a more accurate description) of the locomotive maintenance regime at Reddish depot during 1963. Although it would have been tempting to have included more of the detail from within the record, I have listed here relevant locomotive details from a period spanning 24-hours (lunchtime to lunchtime) during Tuesday 12th and Wednesday 13th March 1963 – a typical 'day' at Reddish depot with eleven electric locomotives dealt with. Besides the aforementioned, the 3-car multiple units and a few of the locally based diesel locomotives were also given attention, many of the latter taking advantage of the depot's wheel lathe.

12th March:

Time	Loco.	Notes.
1315	**26013**	7-day Exam continued.
1315	**27005**	7-day Exam continued.
1015	**26051**	Boiler repairs commence.
1800	**26013**	7-day Exam completed.
1815	**26013**	Brake block bedding run carried out.
1900	**26051**	7-day Exam commences.
2100	**27005**	7-day Exam completed.

13th March:

0030	**27006**	7-day Exam commenced. Completed 0500.
0215	**26050**	7-day Exam commences.
0215	**26051**	7-day Exam and boiler repairs completed.
0230	**26021**	Body washed with 'Esemover' prior to major exam.
0600	**26050**	7-day Exam completed except for boiler items.
0615	**26018**	7-day Exam commences.
0615	**26050**	7-day Exam continued.
0615	**27002**	7-day Exam commences.
1130	**26018**	7-day Exam completed.
1200	**26050**	7-day Exam – boiler items completed.
1230	**27002**	7-day Exam completed.
1315	**27002**	Repairs continue.
1340	**26022**	Message from Control reporting 'hot box' on locomotive which is proceeding to Godley Jct., Guide Bridge and then Reddish.
1630	**26027**	7-day Exam commences.
1630	**26022**	Arrives at depot for repairs – two hot boxes.
1730	**27002**	Repairs completed.
2030	**26046**	Window wiper repairs. Completed 2100.
2100	**26051**	Speedometer repairs commence. Completed 2130.
2115	**26027**	7-day Exam and repairs completed.

A smart looking 26000 TOMMY inside the repair shop at Reddish depot on Sunday 23rd September 1956. The very next day the prototype went into Gorton shops for a Casual Light repair but was out by 11th October. Up to this time 26000 had only accumulated 49,034 miles since receiving a Heavy General overhaul at Stratford in 1952, and only 15,865 miles from that HG up to 8th May 1954 when it was taken into Gorton for major modifications and another HG. *F.W.Hampson (ARPT).*

The Log of 26039 23rd March to 29th August 1962

This six-month record of maintenance examinations carried out on EM1 No.26039 shows the dates and times when the inspections were carried out in 1962. Note that both Reddish and Wath depots were capable of the examinations be they 7, 35 or 140 day events. Each of the EM1 and EM2 electric locomotives were rigorously inspected and records of the inspections were meticulously kept. The high mileages constantly achieved by both classes over the MSW route is a testimony to both the maintenance regime and the staff involved in carrying out the examinations along with the appropriate recording mechanism.

Date	*Time*	*Exam at depot.*
23rd March:	0700–0900	– 7-day Exam Reddish.
26–27th March:	2215–0030	– 7-day Exam Reddish.
31st March:	1815–2030	– 7-day Exam Reddish.
8th April:	0130–0330	– 7-day Exam Wath.
12th April:	0930–1215	– 7-day Exam Wath.
19th–21st April:	1430–1415	– 140-day Exam Wath.
28th April:	1910–2045	– 7-day Exam Wath.
5th May:	0715–1145	– 7-day Exam Wath.
10th May:	1245–1530	– 7-day Exam Wath.
17th May:	0655–0910	– 7-day Exam Wath.
23–24th May:	2230–0515	– 35-day Exam Wath.
31st May:	0630–1115	– 7-day Exam Reddish.
8–9th June:	2215–0030	– 7-day Exam Wath.
29th June:	0800–1630	– 140-day Exam Reddish.
15th June:	1610–1745	– 7-day Exam Wath.
20–21st June:	1030–1230	– 7-day Exam Wath.
5–6th July:	2230–0330	– 7-day Exam Reddish.
12–13th July:	2215–0130	– 7-day Exam Reddish.
26th July:	1545–1750	– 7-day Exam Wath.
3–4th August:	2215–0550	– 35-day Exam Reddish.
9–10th August:	2330–0130	– 7-day Exam Wath.
16th August:	1530–1930	– 7-day Exam Reddish.
24th August:	1910–2110	– 7-day Exam Wath.
29–30th August:	2215–0015	– 7-day Exam Wath.

7-day examinations required inspection and adjustment to: *brake blocks, wind-screen wipers, windows, door handles and catches; motormen's seats; any reported defect.*

140-day exams required inspection and attention where necessary to the following: *bogies and understructure; pantographs; brakes; boiler (where applicable); compressor; exhauster; main motors; carbon brushes on traction motors; auxiliary carbon brushes; relays; batteries; tyres; flanges; all bearings; resistance readings; master controller.*

Besides the three above inspection/examination periods, there were also the following fixed periods to be adhered to for the EM1 and EM2 classes: 70-day; 280-day; 560-day.

(below) **26039 inside the servicing shed at Reddish circa July 1969. Managing at this point to keep hold of the lined Brunswick green livery, the number as yet has no prefix either but a TOPS data panel is attached to the cabside. With discarded brake blocks and rubbish shrewn about the floor, the 'housekeeping' regime appears to be slipping. *Shaw Plan.***

(above) **With 26050, and others for company, last-of-class 26057 stands in the repair shop at Reddish on Sunday 3rd July 1966. Since its HG of 1960, the EM1 has re-acquired some Timken axlebox equipped bogies. This particular road of the depot was the one on which the wheel lathe was located and, at this end of the building too. Capstans and wire-rope hawsers were used to move the locomotives around in this shop but ULYSSES was inside for nothing more than to give a painter a chance of applying the yellow warning panel which had just been freshly painted on that morning. 26057 was taken out of use in early 1977 as 76057, and so that its Timken axlebox bogies could be used on other, less fortunate, members of the class, the body was lifted free of the bogies and then grounded unceremoniously. It was eventually cut up on site at the depot by an outside contractor. However, on this date the locomotive looks splendid enough and the nasty bits of its life were some ten years into the future.** ***A.Ives (ARPT).***

76047 at Crewe on 15th September 1974, after arrival from Reddish. Number painted out, works plate in situ. ***Hugh P.Searle.***

CLASS EM1 (TOPS CLASS 76) The Works Record

Maintaining works:

Until its closure in May 1963, Gorton was the primary workshop for the maintenance of both EM1 and EM2 classes. From 21st April 1963 Crewe works took over the responsibility of overhauling and repairing the two classes. In 1968 the EM2 Co-Cos were withdrawn and stored prior to their sale to Netherlands Railway but the EM1 continued to visit Crewe for all overhauls, both major and minor. The EM1 were classified Class 76 under the BR TOPS scheme. Towards the end of 1972 Crewe was getting rather busy building the new Class 87 electric locomotives for the extension of the WCML electrification and in order to free up space in the Electric traction shop, the Class 76 (whose origins were essentially LNER anyway) were sent, appropriately perhaps, to Doncaster for overhauls. Excepting the odd few which attended Crewe during the period in question, this arrangement continued until September 1975 when the class returned to Crewe on a regular basis and Doncaster ceased to have any further involvement in maintaining the class.
By January 1979, visits to main works appear to have stopped, Reddish depot taking on a further workload to keep the remaining forty members of the class in traffic.
Disappointingly the records covering the period just prior to Gorton's closure, and perhaps more importantly the period when Crewe, and then Doncaster, maintained the MSW motive power, have not surfaced in any of the official archives. Various rumours circulate about the history and record cards being dumped or sold. The only certain thing is that they have not been seen by this writer. Perhaps someone, somewhere, either knows of the existence of the missing history or has the relevant cards in their collection. Whatever the facts are, this compiler would like to know, or perhaps view the said cards in order to 'complete' the history of these iconic locomotives. Because of the missing cards, the latter years of the locomotives' repair histories have been gleaned, in the main, from observations on works visits. Where, at the time, it was not always possible to find out the type of repair being carried out. So, apologies for what might seem to be only half of the story.

Key to symbols used in the tables:
H Heavy overhaul; **HG** Heavy General overhaul; **CH** Casual Heavy overhaul; **CL** Casual Light repair; **NC** Non-Classified repair.
Ss - Serviceable; Su - Un-serviceable; *AB* - Air Brake; *VB* - Vacuum Brake; *CC* - Clear Call; *MU* - Multiple unit working.
< Entered works before that date; > Left works after that date.

This undated illustration shows 26005 in the works yard at Gorton on an unknown date but circa 1956. The paintwork is looking rather tired. This was one of the Ilford gang which returned to the system from exile in 1952. In both 1955 and 1956 it suffered from accident damage and derailment damage respectively and both incidents required Casual Heavy repairs. To say that the MSW electric locomotives were accident prone could be an under statement. ***Norman Preedy.***

26000

Built Doncaster.
To traffic: 4/2/41.
Works No.1914.

LNER No.6701, *renumbered* LNER 6000 – 18/6/46.
BR No.26000 – June 1952, E26000 *by* 7/69.

Repairs:
Doncaster 24/5–25/6/47 **H**;
Stratford 1/4–1/11/52 **HG**;
Gorton 8/5/54–12/5/56 **HG** (15,865 miles) *major modifications*;
Gorton 24/9–11/10/56 **CL** (49,034 miles – since 1/11/52);
Gorton 15/5–8/10/58 **CL** [cost £576];
Gorton 15/9–30/10/59 **CL** (84,828 miles);
Gorton 8/9/60 **NC** (116,042 miles);
Gorton <18/3/62>;
Crewe <25/3–18/4/64;
Crewe <?/11/64>;
Crewe <27/6/65>;
Crewe <24/4–21/5/66;
Taken out of traffic: 2nd March 1968.
Stored (s): 4/3/68–6/69 at Bury;
Re-instated: 21/6/69, *minus nameplates, to passenger service;*
Withdrawn: December 1969, *having run 700,000 miles.*
Re-instated to store at Bury: 11/2/70.
Withdrawn: March 1970. *Still stored at Bury shed 10/4/71.*

The corridor side of 26000. The nameplates were virtually equidistant between the top and bottom of the body, in line with the numbers. This is TOMMY on Sunday 1st March 1953 in a siding at the former Great Central Railway Carriage & Wagon works in Dukinfield; the Bo+Bo had departed from Ilford during the week beforehand. Note that the pantographs have been removed and are probably stored in the attached vans. Of the other EM1s which went to the GE lines, all of them returned to the MSW system with pantographs in place, however, those particular locomotives had travelled north during the latter half of 1952, shortly after 26000 had been taken to Ilford depot from Stratford works. A certain amount of dirt has accumulated on the body of the prototype indicating inside storage had taken place (road dirt picked up in traffic tends to streak or gather in patches). There is no record of 26000 doing any work at Ilford so the more likely probability was storage during the nine months it was resident at the Essex depot. *Norman Preedy.*

(above) **The TOMMY nameplates were positioned somewhat lower on this the non-corridor side of 26000's body. The EM1 is pictured outside Gorton erecting shop on a date unknown in 1953 after its return from Ilford. It has been re-united with its pantographs prior to going into traffic for the first time in the UK. The actual date into traffic is also unknown but TOMMY re-entered Gorton for a two-year sojourn on 8th May 1954 having completed just over 15,000 miles in MSW service. The prototype emerged from Gorton shops and went back into traffic on 12th May 1956 after undergoing a Heavy General overhaul during which major modifications were also carried out. It will be noted that the braking rodding on each bogie served all the wheels unlike the production batch which had indepent brake rods for each wheel.** ***Book Law coll.***
(below) **This illustration from 9th April 1960 allows a comparison to be made between the front ends of the prototype and the production versions of the EM1 class. Besides the radical difference in cabs and the positioning of the front sand boxes, the location and height of the fleet numbers is noticeable too. The cab doors on 26000 are wider than those fitted to the production version but not quite as tall.** ***F.W.Hampson (ARPT).***

TOMMY at Wath on 8th May 1960 along with lined green liveried sister 26018. Up to this time 26000 had run only about 100,000 miles on BR metals, considerably less than any other member of the class due to the inactivity of the locomotive during the period from its arrival back in the UK and two-year long major overhaul and modifications carried out from 1954 to 1956. Here we can see the comparison with the with the different brake rod arrangement to that on the production bogies. *N.W.Skinner*. *(below)* Bereft of nameplates, worksplates, and any hope! E26000 stands on the stub siding by the main entrance to Reddish depot on 27th July 1969. In the background a sister engine has already succumb to cannibalism and is fit only for the breakers' attention. TOMMY was taken out of traffic on 2nd March 1968; put into store at Bury a few days later, and then in July 1969 it was re-instated for passenger service because of shortages amongst the remaining EM1s. E26000 remained operational until the end of December but was re-instated to storage status in January 1970. The inevitable took place during the following March but the seemingly stubborn prototype remained stored at Bury for another year until called into the works at Crewe for scrapping. In November 1972 the deed was done and TOMMY ceased to exist. The chance of saving some real historical metal had been surely missed! *Unknown photographer*.

26001

Built Gorton 1/3/50.
To traffic: 27/10/50.
Works No.1004, *revised to* No.1008.
Painted and lined by 30/9/50 in Gorton paint shop;

Renumbered: E26001 – 20/11/66.
Renumbered: 76001 – 2/74.

Repairs:
Stratford ?/9–4/10/52 **CL**;
Stratford ?/10–1/11/52 *rectify*;
Gorton 24/10–4/11/54 **NC**;
Gorton 12/9–1/10/55 **CL** (56,561 miles);
Gorton 7/11–14/12/57 **CH** (149,320 miles);
Gorton 25/8–3/9/59 **CH** [cost £1,674] (226,306 miles);
Gorton 28/9–9/10/59 **NC** *rectify*;
Gorton 18–19/10/60 **NC** (275,895 miles);
Gorton 22/7–14/9/61 **HG** (308,644 miles);
Gorton 18–22/9/61 **NC** *rectify* (109 miles);
Crewe <9/10–20/11/66;
Crewe <20/12/70–1/2/71>;
Doncaster <1/2/74>;
Doncaster <2/2/75>;
Taken out of traffic: 2/3/68.
Stored (s): 4/3–30/4/68 at Reddish.
Returned to traffic 1/5/68.
Withdrawn: November 1980.

(below) **Showing both sides of the EM1 design to us, along with some rather crowded cabs, Nos.26001 and 26016 were recorded at Penistone on 30th May 1954 having just made history in being the first electric locomotives to work under their own power through the new tunnel at Woodhead. The official opening of the tunnel was still a few days away. Other pictures of this duo taken during the earlier stages of their momentous journey show many more people crowding the cabs. So, it seems that a stop was made at Dunford to allow some of the 'passengerss' to alight in order to give the crews of this pair of EM1s a more comfortable passage to Wath.** ***Book Law coll.***

26001, 26002, and 26003 gathered at Ilford depot in December 1950! Note the tube/cable hanging out of the window but fixed somewhere beneath the body. ***Authors coll.***

Shades of the Ilford depot experience in this illustration (*see also* 26002). However, we have moved on twenty-five years to Wednesday 30th March 1977 and 76001 was now amongst friends. The class leader since 1970, this EM1 did not quite make it to the very end and was withdrawn in November 1980. As 26001, it nearly didn't make it to 1970 when it was stored unserviceable in July 1968 only to be re-instated some two months later. ***Norman Preedy.***

26002

Built Gorton 30/3/50.
To traffic: 27/10/50.
Works No.1005, *revised to* No.1009.
Still in primer on 30/9/50 inside Gorton paint shop.
Returned to traffic: 16/3/52.

Renumbered: E26002 – ?/?
Renumbered: 76002 – 4/74.

Repairs:
Gorton 2–17/3/56 **CH** (127,373 miles);
Gorton 13–25/6/56 **CH** (138,923 miles);
Gorton 27/6–8/9/56 **CH** (138,959 miles);
Gorton 15/10/58–11/3/59 **HG** [cost £3,233] (229,417 miles);
Gorton 16/2–16/3/60 **CL** [cost £202] (40,864 miles);
Gorton 28–30/9/60 **NC** (62,265 miles);
Gorton <3–6/2/62;
Crewe <17/10–16/11/65>;
Crewe <22/2/74–17/5/74;
Taken out of traffic: 2/3/68.
Into store: Reddish 4/3/68–?/?
Re-instated: ?/?
Into store: Reddish 7/77–6/78.
Withdrawn: 6/78.

26002 shows off its corridor side in 1956 whilst stabled at Reddish. The polished metal finish front window frames appear to be standing up well to the rigours of the Woodhead route weather but the fact that most of their working lives were spent away from the spoiling nature of steam locomotive smoke must have helped the cause. *L.Turnbull.*

Between 27th October 1950 and 17th March 1951, ten EM1s (Nos.26001 to 26010) were sent from Gorton, as they were completed, to Ilford so that they could at least be run-in and also tried and tested on the GE suburban lines which were already energised for 1500v d.c. This is 26002 on one such turn with nine empty coaches at Chadwell Heath on Sunday 5th November 1950. Note that only the rear pantograph is raised as current collection tests were being conducted. It was initially planned that the MSW locomotives would only be required to run with a rear pantograph raised but dirty contacts, along with ice on the wires in winter over the Woodhead line meant that both pantographs had to be used. There is that tube/cable again – obviously something to do with the tests. *Authors coll.*

Forlorn, unloved, and certainly unwanted! EM1s Nos.26002, 26001, and 26003 are out in the cold at Ilford depot on Wednesday 6th December 1950. *Transport Treasury.*

Standing on the siding which runs along the south wall of the erecting shop at Gorton, 26002 appears ready for a Monday morning departure in this illustration recorded on Sunday 4th February 1962. In the left background can be seen the north wall of Beyer, Peacocks erecting shop which at this time was in the throes of building Hymek B-B diesel-hydraulics for the Western Region. *George Watson.*

26003

Built Gorton 22/4/50.
To traffic: 15/11/50.
Works No.1006, *revised to* No.1010.

Renumbered: E26003 – 6/68.
Renumbered: 76003 – 3/72.
Renumbered: 76036 – 10/76.

Repairs:
Gorton 29/7–13/8/55 **CH** (58,932 miles);
Gorton 19/2–4/5/57 **CH** (134,557 miles);
Gorton 9–25/2/59 **CH** [cost £1,203] (215,959 miles);
Gorton 22/3–11/5/60 **HG** [cost £3,437] (262,513 miles);
Gorton 20–24/5/60 **CL** (854 miles);
Gorton 13–14/9/60 **NC** (13,784 miles);
Crewe <9/6/68>;
Crewe <30/1–?/3/72>;
Crewe <4/11/76 **HG**, *AB, CC and MU fitted;*
Crewe <25/9/77, *VB removed 9/77 (dA).*
Taken out of traffic: 2/3/68.
Into Store: Reddish 4/3/68–30/4/68.
Returned to traffic: 1/5/68.
Into Store: Reddish August 1980 Ss.
Withdrawn: July 1981.

(below) **En route to the MSW line! 26003 was safely tucked into a northbound freight passing through Cambridge on Friday 18th July 1952 whilst returning home from Essex. Next stop March, then transit of the GE/GN Joint line to Doncaster, over to Mexborough for the final leg to Wath and overhead wires! Sister No.26001 could not be repatriated until November because it had been involved in an unrecorded incident which saw it having to enter the works at Stratford in September for a Casual Light repair (the usual classification for accident damage repairs requiring minimal to moderate attention).** ***Transport Treasury.***
(bottom) **26003 approaches Guide Bridge with a service from Manchester (London Road) on an unrecorded date in the 1950s. On the left is the branch to Stockport where what appears to be an A5 tank is waiting for a westbound service from Hull which it would take as far as Manchester (Central) via the Fallowfield loop line. Dead ahead are the four lines to Audenshaw whilst branching off to the right is the line to Ashton Moss.** ***J.W.Armstrong (ARPT).***

26004

Built Gorton 5/50.
To traffic: 14/2/51.
Works No.1007, *revised to* No.1011.

Renumbered: E26004 – 4/66.
Renumbered: 76004 – 2/74.

Repairs:
Gorton 23–30/4/55 **CH** (40,679 miles);
Gorton 31/3–15/9/56 **CH** (80,941 miles);
Gorton 30/10–12/11/58 **CH** [cost £1,078] (179,284 miles);
Gorton 18/1–9/3/60 **HG** [cost £3,789] (234,079 miles);
Gorton 29/10–1/11/60 **NC** (27,992 miles);
Crewe <15/2/64>;
Crewe <24/4/66>;
Crewe <1/2/71>;
Taken out of traffic: 2/3/68.
Into store: Reddish 4/3–30/4/68.
Returned to traffic: 1/5/68.
Withdrawn: February 1977.
Re-instated: August 1977 (*apparently working during March*).
Stored again *by* 3rd September 1977.
Withdrawn: June 1978.

(below) **The clatter of empty 16-ton mineral wagons made much more noise than the motive power on the Woodhead route. 26004, in lined green livery and with a yellow warning panel, runs easily through Torside and up 'the bank' towards Woodhead with eastbound empties circa 1966. *Transport Treasury.*** *(bottom)* **76004 is stabled at Guide Bridge SP on Tuesday 19th March 1974 in a position where it was not quite coupled-up to other members of the class. Being vacuum-only fitted during its lifetime saw its work potential decrease with each passing year as more air-braked rolling stock replaced non-fitted or vacuum fitted stock. Its untimely end took place in June 1978, more than three years before the majority were withdrawn, but by some measure of irony, and some unwanted materials inside its bodywork, 76004 was amongst the very last to be cut up. *Norman Preedy.***

26005

Built Gorton 26/5/50.
To traffic: 25/1/51.
Works No.1008, *revised to* No.1012.

Renumbered: E26005 – 6/66.

Repairs:
Gorton 24/1–26/3/55 **CH** *collision damage* (38,007 miles);
Gorton 25/1–10/2/56 **CH** *derailment* (74,376 miles);
Gorton 10/11–1/12/56 **CH** (110,062 miles);
Gorton 27/8–25/9/58 **CH** [cost £1,276] (191,777 miles);
Gorton 29–31/12/59 **CL** [cost £1,441] (250,945 miles);
Gorton 29–30/8/60 **NC** (281,318 miles);
Gorton 14/9–24/11/61 **HG** (325,748 miles);
Gorton <3/3/63>;
Crewe <10/11/63>;
Crewe <3/5/64>;
Crewe <4/10/64>;
Crewe <20–29/5/66>;
Stored Su: 7/68;
Taken out of store 7/69 *(storage venue unknown);*
Withdrawn: March 1970, at Reddish;
Crewe 24/7/70 for c/u?; *Stabled in works arrival sidings 20/12/70, taken into Electric Traction shop by 14/3/71 for cannibalising. Hulk cut up June 1971.*

(below) **In amongst its internal combustion cousins, 26005 is the solitary electric locomotive in the works yard at Crewe on an unknown date in 1966 (it was observed there in May 1966). A yellow warning panel has been acquired but the Bo+Bo appears to have just arrived at Crewe because road dirt is ingrained. Withdrawal in March 1970 prevented this EM1 from receiving its TOPS number which would have been 76005. Including 26005, and TOMMY, some eight members of the class were condemned before the TOPS renumbering was introduced. *Transport Treasury.***

(above) **Bound for Wath yard, 26005 and an unidentified sister restart a long train of mineral empties from the refuge at Penistone West on 26th June 1954.** ***K.R.Pirt.***

(below) **A section of the 'weekend sojourn' at Wath – 17th July 1955.** ***K.R.Pirt.***

(above) **Nearly there! 26005 gives a final push to a westbound mixed freight which it was banking on the Worsborough branch in May 1956. The continuous movement of freight over this section of railway was one of the main reasons for electrifying the MSW line. Note the adjustable cross beams of the catenary which could altered to suit any mining subsidence problems suffered in this area.** ***Transport Treasury.***

(below) **Captured on film during the afternoon of Sunday 7th October 1962, a nice pair of lined green liveried examples, 26005 and 26038, take a weekend rest at Wath.** ***Unknown photographer.***

26006

Built Gorton 15/6/50.
To traffic: 25/1/51.
Works No.1009, *revised to* No.1013.

Renumbered: E25006 – 2/67.
Renumbered: 76006 – 1/74.

Repairs:
Gorton 1–15/10/55 **CH** (49,968 miles);
Gorton 16/11/56–5/1/57 **CH** (103,922 miles);
Gorton 26/1–19/2/59 **CH** [cost £1,119] (201,029 miles);
Gorton 9/1–11/3/61 **HG** [cost £3,603] (289,143 miles);
Gorton 26/5–12/6/61 **CH** (8,033 miles);
Gorton 14–21/8/61 **CL** (14,573 miles);
Crewe <25/3–3/4/64>;
Crewe <22/1/67>;
Crewe <10/10–9/11/69 **HG**, *AB, CC and MU fitted* ;
Doncaster <1/1/74>;
Reddish <9/79> **CL** *and repaint*;
Withdrawn: July 1981.

(below) **In transit from Essex to Mexborough, 26006 paused at Cambridge on Friday 25th July 1952. The exiles from Gorton were going back home to more familiar territory and to start some work. The EM1 still retains a slight sheen to its bodywork more than eighteen months after being 'put into traffic' to do basically nothing except a few road tests and then spend over a year in storage. Nearly thirty years of operations lay before 26006 at this stage of its life and BR were going to get their worth out of this considerable investment. *Transport Treasury*.** *(bottom)* **Virtually ex-works, 76006 stables at Guide Bridge on Wednesday 21st August 1974 with similarly MU-fitted 76010. Both of these locomotives attended the shops at Doncaster for overhauls during the short period when the former LNER 'Plant' works took over maintenance of the class. 76006 however has come back with just the drivers side of the cabs 'numbered' and with the double arrow symbol in the lower position – the Doncaster preference it seems! 76010 visited the year before and managed to retain numbers in all four cab side locations. *Norman Preedy*.**

26007

Built Gorton 30/6/50.
To traffic: 14/2/51.
Works No.1010 *revised to* No.1014.

Renumbered: E26007 – 22/6/69.
Renumbered: 76007 – 2/74.

Repairs:
Gorton 27/9–9/10/54 **NC**;
Gorton ?/12/54–12/1/55 **CH**;
Gorton 8–12/11/55 **NC** (67,185 miles);
Gorton 20/4–18/5/57 **CL** (136,330 miles);
Gorton 29/9–17/10/58 **CH** [cost £1,410] (197,460 miles);
Gorton 9–14/1/60 **CH** [cost £1,673] (255,694 miles);
Gorton 4–6/10/60 **NC** (286,382 miles);
Gorton 10/8–19/10/61 **HG** (322,988 miles);
Crewe <29/5/66>;
Crewe 30/3–22/6/69 **HG**, *AB, CC and MU fitted*;
Crewe <22/2/74–17/5/74;
Withdrawn: July 1981.

(below) **26007 and 26027 at the south end of Wath depot, 8th August 1954. The industrial waste forming the tip on this eastern side of the shed gives an indication of the amount of fill required to create the necessary ground area on which to build the shed and the associated yards. As mentioned in the text, Wath shed was built with future colliery subsidence in mind. *Unknown photographer.*** *(bottom)* **76007 stabled at Reddish and MU-coupled to 76024 on Wednesday 16th March 1977. The two different types of axleboxes shared amongst the class can be seen in use. This illustration also shows off well the small square hole cut into the top of the cab side sheets for ventilation purposes. The narrowness of the cab doors is also shown to advantage; it was a myth that all MSW Motormen were slim but it certainly helped when they were! Note the TOPS information box is located below the centre of the number, as normal, whereas 76024 has its information box positioned beneath the right side of the number. 76007's double arrow is in the upper – Crewe – position. 76022, another MU fitted engine, peeps in from the left of frame. *Norman Preedy.***

26008

Built Gorton 29/7/50.
To traffic: 17/3/51.
Works No.1011 *revised to* No.1015.

Renumbered: E26008 – 18/5/69.
Renumbered: 76008 – 11/72.

Repairs:
Gorton 18–30/8/54 **NC**;
Gorton 19/10–5/11/55 **CH** (61,759 miles);
Gorton 10/2–16/6/56 **CH** (75,244 miles);
Gorton 12/9–19/10/57 **CL** (124,905 miles);
Gorton 27/12/57–8/2/58 **CH** [cost £1,893] (134,081 miles);
Gorton 19–26/6/58 **NC** (151,432 miles);
Gorton 17–20/11/59 **CH** [cost £1,421] (213,708 miles);
Gorton 9–13/1/60 **CL** (220,559 miles);
Gorton 24/4/60 **NC** (264,250 miles);
Gorton 19–23/12/60 **NC**;
Gorton 23/5–8/7/61 **HG** (283,219 miles); *Green.*
Crewe <7–16//11/65>;
Crewe <21/7–29/9/68>;
Crewe 3/11/68–18/5/69 **HG**, *AB, MU fitted, blue*;
Crewe 23/5–27/7/69 *Rectification*;
Crewe <12/10–1/12/72>;
Withdrawn: July 1981.

(opposite) **The continuing movement of coal from south Yorkshire and north Nottinghamshire into the industrial and domestic fires of Lancashire was the reason behind the electrification of the Woodhead route. This picture of a rather cold March day in 1958 reveals one of the railheads where the electric traction took over the coal trains from the steam motive power. This is Orgreave where remnants of snow cling onto the far embankment as 26008 departs for the west with a loaded coal train. Steam is evident as are other EM1s waiting for their next trip 'over the top'. It appears that by this time the brightly polished horizontal handrail and front window frames had become the norm for the class.** ***W.R.E.Lewis.*** *(opposite, bottom)* **Now in blue livery with full yellow ends, not to mention the MU equipment, E26008 stands in the works yard at Crewe on 18th May 1969. The nearest worksplate has been removed; to accommodate the TOPS panel or to add to a collection somewhere?** ***Norman Preedy.***

With its cab looking somewhat cleaner, brighter and fresher than the rest of the locomotive, 26008 looks as though it has recently had works attention for accident damage; note also the door which has not yet received a top coat of paint. In actuality, 26008 had just received a Casual Heavy repair and was still under works care. The EM1 is stabled on the Up siding at the east end of Guide Bridge station on Friday 15th June 1956. ***Norman Preedy.***

26008

E26008

26009

Built Gorton 11/8/50.
To traffic: 17/3/51.
Works No.1012 *revised to* No.1016.

Renumbered: E26009 – *by* 27/9/68.
Renumbered: 76009 – 2/74.

Repairs:
Stratford ?/10–29/11/52 *Rectification*;
Gorton 12–15/10/54 **NC**;
Gorton 24/9–15/10/55 **CH** (61,890 miles);
Gorton 17/2–9/3/57 **CH** (128,959 miles);
Gorton 30/3–18/4/59 **CH** [cost £1,496] (224,872 miles);
Gorton 8/8–23/9/60 **HG** [cost £2,494] (282,611 miles);
Crewe 25/3–3/4/64>;
Crewe <4/10/64>;
Crewe 29/5–24/7/66>;
Crewe <27/9/68>;
Crewe <26/4/70> **HG**, *AB, CC and MU fitted*;
Doncaster <1/2/74>;
Doncaster <4–26/5/75>;
Withdrawn: July 1981.

MU fitted E26009 in blue with full yellow ends but still retaining the BR crest. Guide Bridge SP, 21st March 1973. ***Norman Preedy.***

26010

Built Gorton 24/8/50.
To traffic: 17/3/51.
Works No.1013 *revised to* No.1017.

Renumbered: E26010 – 15/12/68.
Renumbered: 76010 – 2/73.

Repairs:
Stratford <?/10–1/11/52 *Rectification;*
Gorton 25–29/10/54 **NC**;
Gorton 19–28/5/55 **CL** (48,225 miles);
Gorton 15/9–6/10/56 **CH** (105,810 miles);
Gorton 10/2–19/3/59 **CH** [cost £1,345] (211,273 miles);
Gorton 27/9–9/11/60 **HG** [cost £3,342] (279,444 miles);
Crewe <21/7–29/9/68>;
Crewe 3/11/68–?/2/69>**HG**, *AB, CC and MU fitted*;
Crewe <11/12/69>;
Doncaster <2/2/73>;
Withdrawn: July 1981.

(below) **Time for some fast running on passenger workings! 26010, still wearing that rather dull finish afforded many of the class in the late Fifties', comes to a halt at Sheffield (Victoria) in July 1959 after a run over from Manchester. Again the bright finish of the horizontal handrail and the front window frames is notable. *A.R.Thompson (ARPT).***

26011

Built Gorton 9/9/50.
To traffic: 31/5/51.
Works No.1014 *revised to* No.1018.

Renumbered: E26011 *by* 11/68.
Renumbered: 76011 – 7/73.

Repairs:
Gorton 20/4–25/7/52 **CH** (6,898 miles);
Gorton 9/11–13/11/54 **CL** (67,503 miles);
Gorton 14/9–20/10/56 **CH** (150,642 miles);
Gorton 9–11/2/57 **NC**;
Gorton 2/9–26/10/57 **CH** (188,371 miles);
Gorton 27/3–5/4/58 **CL** [cost £31];
Gorton 28/7–7/8/59 **CH** [cost £1,628] (269,906 miles);
Gorton 21–23/9/60 **NC** (318,689 miles);
Gorton 23/1–16/3/61 **HG** [cost £3,088] (334,415 miles);
Gorton <14/10/62>;
Crewe <14/6/64>;
Crewe 3/11/68–30/1/69 **HG**, *AB, CC and MU fitted*;
Doncaster <5/5–1/7/73> **CH**;
Withdrawn: July 1981.

(below) **With the erecting shop forming the background of this illustration, 26011 stood on the yard at Gorton works on Sunday 23rd September 1956 looking rather weather beaten. The EM1 had already been 'on works' for a week awaiting entry to the shops for a Casual Heavy overhaul after covering 150,000 miles since new, the bulk of them totted up during the previous two years of full electric operations on the MSW. 26011 eventually emerged on Saturday 20th October 1956, still in black livery. *F.W.Hampson.*** *(bottom)* **26011 outside Wath shed on 7th October 1962. By now the EM1 has acquired lined green livery, and a set of Timken axlebox equipped bogies, all courtesy of a Heavy General overhaul at Gorton from 23rd January to 16th March during the previous year. It was about to visit the works at Gorton again during the week following this illustration being captured on film. *F.W. Hampson (ARPT).***

(above) **26011 on Sunday 8th May 1960 at Wath! Note the small version of the BR lion-and-wheel emblem which was applied in 1956. Also, it is worth noting the bright finish of the horizontal handrail wrapped around the cab along with the front window frames. In later years the members fitted with MU gear had their handrails lifted (bent upwards) at the front ends by giving them an upward slant at the transition point between the sides and front, so as to clear the MU connections. The original vacuum braked locomotives were unaffected. *N.W.Skinner*.** *(below)* **Stabled at Rotherwood on 7th March 1981, No.76011 has retained the Timken roller bearing bogies acquired almost twenty years previously. They would remain with the EM1 to the scrapyard. *Norman Preedy*.**

26012

Built Gorton 20/9/50.
To traffic: 7/5/51.
Works No.1015 *revised to* No.1019.

Renumbered: E26012 – 12/67.
Renumbered: 76012 – 4/73.

Repairs:
Wath ?/6–5/7/52 **CL**;
Gorton 13–27/3/54 **CH** (53,087 miles);
Gorton 18/11–3/12/55 **CH** (115,531 miles);
Gorton 26/10–30/11/57 **CH** (207,406 miles);
Gorton 20/5–2/6/59 **CH** [cost £1,851] (278,127 miles);
Gorton 14/9/60 **NC** (339,042 miles);
Gorton 19/10–1/12/60 **HG** [cost £3,064] (342,867 miles);
Crewe <10/11/63>;
Crewe <24/4/65>;
Crewe 24/11/67>;
Crewe 7/11–18/12/69 **HG**, *AB, CC and MU fitted*;
Crewe 21/8/70>;
Doncaster <4/2–5/3/73>;
Withdrawn: July 1981.

(below) **A nice broadside of 76012 running through Dewsnap and passing the former Great Central Railway carriage and wagon works on 11th June 1979. It was at those workshops where the EM1s were equipped with all the electrical gear and motors. *Norman Preedy.*** *(bottom)* **76012 at Wath during the final months of operations on the MSW. *S.Carter.***

26013

Built Gorton 12/10/50.
To traffic: 31/5/51.
Works No.1016 *revised to* No.1020.

Renumbered: E26013 – 5/66.
Renumbered: 76013 – 9/72.

Repairs:
Gorton 25/7–8/11/52 **CL** (13,435 miles);
Gorton 6–22/10/55 **CH** (102,073 miles);
Gorton 11/2–2/3/57 **CH** (164,784 miles);
Gorton 29/1–24/4/59 **HG** [cost £3,422] (251,666 miles);
Gorton 6–22/11/60 **NC** (72,677 miles);
Gorton <14/10/62>;
Crewe 14/6/64>;
Crewe <24/4/66>;
Crewe <5/3/67>;
Crewe 22/2–18/4/70 **HG**, *AB, CC and MU fitted*;
Crewe <6/8/72>;
Withdrawn: July 1981.

Members of the RCTS clamber around the cab of 26013 at Penistone to get what was probably their first glimpse inside the 'operating floor' of an EM1. The throng some 230 participants had arrived at the South Yorkshire junction aboard the RCTS *SOUTH YORKSHIRE No.2* rail tour on 7th June 1953 from Sheffield (Midland), the Bo+Bo being their motive power from Elsecar junction to Penistone via Worsborough. This special was apparently only the second passenger working to have ascended the bank under electric power (the first was a press run on 31st January 1952). *K.H.Cockerill (ARPT).*

Star for the day, 26013 poses for the numerous photographers which have arrived aboard the RCTS special. Not a high visibility jacket in sight it will be noted, or a railway policeman. Casualties that day, from all forms of accident – Nil! Happy days! *K.H.Cockerill (ARPT).* *(below)* **Having run round its five coach train, made up of ex-LMS saloon coaches, and now safely coupled up and ready for the return working, 26013 is once again the centre of attention before taking the 'excursionists' to Wombwell exchange sidings where 'Director' No.62667 SOMME took over for the indirect return journey to Midland station. According to the itinerary, twelve minutes were allowed arrival to departure at Penistone; slick work from both the railway authorities and the photographers. *K.H.Cockerill (ARPT).***

En route to Penistone. Traversing the Worsborough bank and seen near Kendall Green crossing, 26013 and the RCTS rail tour created a little bit of history and what's more, it is now pure history. *C.J.B.Sanderson (ARPT).* *(below)* **With the end virtually in sight, 76013 underwent servicing and some cosmetic surgery at Reddish on Sunday 14th June 1981. Note that besides the worksplates being refitted, the Metro-Vic plate has also been put back to its rightful position. With all that brass knocking about, one can only assume that another railtour was in the offing! *Norman Preedy.***

26014

Built Gorton 25/10/50.
To traffic: 22/5/51.
Works No.1017 *revised to* No.1021.

Renumbered: E26014 – 6/67.
Renumbered: 76014 – 2/74.

Repairs:
Gorton 2–7/6/54 **CH** (52,468 miles);
Gorton 5–12/3/55 **CH** (84,121 miles);
Gorton 9–23/4/55 **CL** (87,504 miles);
Gorton 11/1–2/2/57 **CH** (167,661 miles);
Gorton 3–6/2/58 **NC**;
Gorton 19/2–1/3/58 **CL** [cost £924] (217,585 miles);
Gorton 7/4–19/6/59 **HG** [cost £3,799] (267,844 miles);
Gorton 25/8/60 **NC** (50,251 miles);
Gorton 27–28/9/60 **CL** (53,309 miles);
Crewe <21/2/65>;
Crewe 19/3–20/6/67;
Crewe 8/3–28/4/70 **HG**, *AB, CC and MU fitted*;
Crewe <9/8/74–23/9/74>;
Withdrawn: July 1981.

(below) **26014 outside Gorton erecting shop on 28th April 1951. The EM1 has just returned from Dukinfield after installation of the various electrical components and is about to undergo its final testing prior to entering traffic some three weeks hence followed by a special appointment in York (*see* later). *Norman Preedy*.** *(bottom)* **E26014 with no discernible BR crest, and sister 76015 with everything, run past Godley Junction signal box in March 1973. *Norman Preedy*.**

26015

Built Gorton 8/11/50.
To traffic: 26/7/51.
Works No.1018 *revised to* No.1022.

Renumbered: E26015 – 5/65.
Renumbered: 76015 – 11/72

Repairs:
Gorton 31/10–7/11/53 **CH** (47,473 miles);
Gorton 16–30/7/55 **CL** (106,258 miles);
Gorton 11–18/6/56 **CH** (147,895 miles);
Gorton 19/2–23/3/57 **CH** (181,086 miles);
Gorton 5/8–24/12/58 **HG** [cost £3,995] (245,301 miles);
Gorton 20–27/4/60 **CH** [cost £1,288] (60,424 miles);
Gorton 9/9/60 **NC** (75,063 miles);
Crewe 21/2–16/5/65;
Crewe 12/12/69–27/1/70 **HG**, *AB, CC and MU fitted*;
Crewe <3–12/11/72>;
Crewe <25/1/76>;
Crewe 2/4/76>;
Withdrawn: July 1981.

This is the earliest illustration we can offer of 26015 but at least it is the original locomotive just renumbered for TOPS as 76015. Wath, circa 1977. *Brian North.*

26016

Built Gorton 17/11/50.
To traffic: 25/7/51.
Works No.1019 *revised to* No.1023.

Renumbered: E26016 – 24/2/69.
Renumbered: 76016 – 6/3/73.

Repairs:
Gorton 22–25/9/54 **CH** (67,014 miles);
Gorton 15/6–7/7/56 **CH** (146,330 miles);
Gorton 24/12/57–8/2/58 **CH** (213,731 miles);
Gorton 13/2–9/5/58 **CH** [cost £1,734];
Gorton 21/11/59–12/1/60 **HG** [cost £3,270] (295,053 miles);
Gorton 20–21/1/60 **NC** *Rectify*;
Gorton 15–16/12/60 **NC** (39,249 miles);
Crewe 10/11/63–18/12/63>,
Crewe <15–29/9/68>;
Crewe <3/11/68–24/2/69 **HG**, *AB, MU fitted, blue*;
Doncaster <4/2–6/3/73>;
Crewe <23/1/74>;
Withdrawn: July 1981.

Sunday 2nd March 1958 and EM1s are lined up ready to journey westward with what was then regarded as the most important commodity in the British economy – coal. This 'interchange' from steam to electric haulage and located east of Sheffield, handled much of the coal from the South Yorkshire and Nottinghamshire pits. The newly applied lined green livery on 26016 has not emphasised the horizontal handrails or the front window frames which are now the same colour as the bodywork. *W.R.E.Lewis (ARPT).*

26016 lining up for examination at Reddish depot on 3rd July 1966, along with sister 26041 and Co-Co 27002. It will be noticed that by now all three locomotives have the square cut ventilation holes above the side windows of the cabs. Like any locomotive type, the EM1s and EM2s were subject to ongoing alterations and improvements throughout their lives; cab ventilation was one such improvement. *A.Ives (ARPT).*

(below) **Crewe 23rd February 1969: E26016 is ready to enter traffic after a major overhaul and the fitting of MU equipment. The microphone of the 'Clear Call' system can be seen throughthe nearest cab window. The 'Clear Call' experiments had started in the late 1950s and was a means of communication whereby crews in separate locomotives, double heading or banking, working the same train could talk to each other by way of a telephone system using the overhead wires as a carrier. British Thompson Houston had equipped six of the EM1s with such but it was deemed to be something of a failure at that time and horn communication was resorted to in the meantime. With the introduction of the Merry-Go-Round coal trains in the late Sixties' it became something of a necessity to have cab-to-cab communications between the train engines and the banking engines and A.E.I. came up with a 'better' system in 1969. However, the first tests showed little improvement over those carried out during the previous decade but once adjustments had been made, the AEI system worked perfectly and was adopted for the Class 76s in 1970. Why E26016 was so equipped in early 1969 when the experiments did not apparently proceed until later in the year is unknown; this particular engine was also not one of those equipped for the tests anyway! Note the nicely touched-up Timken axlebox covers and all those MU connections. *Norman Preedy.***

26017

Built Gorton 29/11/50.
To traffic: 31/7/51.
Works No.1020 *revised to* No.1024.

Renumbered: E26017 – 10/66.

Repairs:
Gorton 5–12/8/54 **CH** (63,507 miles);
Gorton 28/5–11/6/55 **CH** (97,741 miles);
Gorton 28/8–13/10/56 **CH** (151,295 miles);
Gorton 15–19/2/57 **NC**;
Gorton 21/6–14/9/57 **CH** (183,759);
Gorton 11–17/9/59 **CH** [cost £1,480] (274,243 miles);
Gorton 31/8–3/9/60 **NC** (314,985 miles);
Gorton <8/4/61>**HG**; *Green.*
Crewe <22/6/63>;
Crewe <15/2/64>;
Crewe 11/9–9/10/66>;
To store Su: *(accident damage)* at Reddish *after* 19/2/70;
Withdrawn: March 1970, at Reddish.

Ex works! 26017 stabled on the stub siding by the main gate at Reddish depot in September 1957. Green livery and lined-out, the Bo+Bo looked every bit a dandy. Note 'EM1' painted on the bufferbeam; an LNER practice perpetuated by Gorton right up to closure of that workshop in 1963. *P.J.Robinson.*

26018

Built Gorton ?/12/50.
To traffic: 5/9/51.
Works No.1021 *revised to* No.1025.

Renumbered: E26018 – 5/67;
Renumbered: 76018 – 2/74;
Renumbered: 76035 – 6/76;

Repairs:
Gorton 17–23/9/54 **CH** (67,368 miles);
Gorton 18/2–3/3/56 **CH** (128,245 miles);
Gorton 9/1–15/2/58 **CH** [cost £1,096] (216,107 miles);
Gorton 25/11/59–4/2/60 **HG** [cost £4,063] (300,188 miles);
Gorton 7–9/11/61 **NC** (76,144 miles);
Gorton <3/3/63>;
Crewe <26/1/64>;
Crewe 19/2–19/3/67>;
Crewe <27/6/71>;
Crewe 5/12/75–4/6/76> **HG**; *AB, CC and MU fitted, VB removed.*
Reddish <16/9/79> *lifted off bogies and receiving attention;*
Withdrawn: July 1981.

(below) **26018, in the original black livery and large BR emblem, stands at the south end of Reddish depot on Sunday 23rd September 1956. *Unknown photographer.*** *(bottom)* **Though having nothing to do with steam locomotives in its formative years, Wath depot eventually took on an allocation of diesel locomotives once Mexborough engine shed began its run down to closure. Mainly Brush Type 2s, but also English Electric Type 3s and BR Sulzer Type 2s, were allocated and Wath even gained a shed code of its own – 41C – but none of the EM1s were ever officially allocated, except in the early years when Wath was regarded as a sub shed of Mexborough. This November 1962 illustration captured by Ian Coulson reveals 26018 and 26042 sharing stabling room with newly delivered Brush diesel-electric D5862 of Darnall depot. *I.W.Coulson.***

Charging up the air tanks and fresh from overhaul at Crewe, E26018 shows off the new prefix, blue body livery, and yellow warning panel. The new era for EM1 livery had already commenced a few months beforehand but this pristine example standing in the overcast drizzle of Manchester on 14th May 1967 looks rather nice. *A.Ives (ARPT).* *(below)* **Masquerading as 76035, this is really 26018/76018 at Orgreave on 19th March 1977. Renumbered 76018 from E26018 in February 1974, the EM1 was renumbered again during June 1976 to tidy up the number grouping of the MU fitted examples. The real 26035 was condemned in March 1970 – following accident damage in 1968 – and cut up at Reddish by contractors in October 1971. *Norman Preedy.***

26019

Built Gorton 21/12/50.
To traffic: 25/9/51.
Works No.1022 *revised to* No.1026.

Renumbered: E26019 – 9/67;

Repairs:
Wath 2–5/7/52 **NC**;
Gorton 15/8–11/12/54 **CH** *accident damage, derailment* (41,617 miles);
Gorton 23–26/2/55 **NC** (47,184 miles);
Gorton 14–18/6/55 **CL** (62,642 miles);
Gorton 11–14/8/56 **NC**;
Gorton 17/11–8/12/56 **CH** (128,654 miles);
Gorton 8–27/9/58 **CH** [cost £1,042] (208,685 miles);
Gorton 28/11–19/12/58 **CH** (216,850 miles);
Gorton 12–13/10/60 **NC** (300,080 miles);
Gorton 8/12/60–26/1/61 **HG** (306,750 miles);
Gorton <1/9/62>;
Crewe <27/8/67>;
Withdrawn: October 1971 (*active until 6th October!*).
Cut up at Crewe April 1972.

26019 stables at the south end of the servicing shed at Reddish in the early Sixties'. *N.E.Stead coll.*

26020

Built Gorton 17/2/51.
To traffic: 17/2/51.
Works No.1023 *revised to* No.1027.

Renumbered: E26020 – ?/67.
Renumbered: 76020 – 6/73.

Repairs:
Wath 28/6–5/7/52 **NC**;
Gorton 23/5–12/9/53 **CH** (34,960);
Gorton 8/1–5/2/55 **CH** (36,100 miles);
Gorton 10/5/55 **NC**;
Gorton 29/1–23/2/57 **CH** (127,298 miles);
Gorton 25/9–1/10/58 **CL** [cost £426] (199,493 miles);
Gorton 24/6–22/9/59 **HG** [cost £4,120] (235,753 miles);
Gorton 2–3/11/61 **NC** (94,363 miles);
Gorton <1/9/62>;
Crewe <10/11/63>;
Crewe <2–30/1/66; *Blue*.
Doncaster <6/5–1/6/73>;
Crewe <24/11/74>;
Into store: Reddish 7/77.
Withdrawn: August 1977 *for preservation*.
Into Doncaster works for painting. Resident in paint shop there until 29/8/78 when it was hauled to the NRM as EM1 No.26020, via Healey Mills, on 30/8/78 by 31106.

Celebrity 26020 looking rather bland at Reddish depot on 3rd July 1966 after a visit to Crewe earlier in the year where it lost its lined green livery to this insipid blue. Note also that the train heating connections had been removed on that visit to Crewe, along with the boiler; that appliance had been fitted in February 1955. For its preservation within the National Collection, a boiler was refitted at Reddish in July 1977. The EM1 is alongside a pair of the depot's Matterson lifting jacks which could easily accommodate the body of an EM1 or EM2 (or any of the BR diesels) so that bogies could be easily removed. *A.Ives (ARPT).*

26021

Built Gorton 6/1/51.
To traffic: 2/10/51.
Works No.1024 *revised to* No.1028.

Renumbered: E26021 – 14/6/66.
Renumbered: 76021 – 6/73.

Repairs:
Gorton 6/4–7/5/52 **CL** (8,246 miles);
Gorton 23/5–8/8/53 **CH** (31,726 miles);
Gorton 18–30/8/54 **CH** (57,488 miles);
Gorton 14/10–17/11/56 **CH** (147,272 miles);
Gorton 31/12/58–3/4/59 **HG** [cost £3,671] (246,849 miles);
Gorton 5–7/10/60 **NC** (65,402 miles);
Gorton <14/10/62>;
Crewe <14/6/64>;
Crewe <24/4–14/6/66, *blue*;
Crewe <?/5–23/6/69 **HG**, *AB, CC and MU fitted*;
Doncaster <6/5/73>;
Withdrawn: July 1981.

(below) **The single lining on black liveried 26021 is discernible in this undated but 'early days' view at Wath. This aspect of the shed at wath reveals the fragility of the lightweight cladding materials employed. *N.E.Stead coll.*** *(bottom)* **26021 and 26029 offer us both sides of the class for comparison in this undated view at Wath circa 1955. The non-corridor side of 26021 reveals the position of the BR emblem to be quite far back from the middle of the locomotive whilst the corridor side of 26029 shows the lion-and-wheel to be just off centre to the right. The MV works plate was located dead centre on the EM1s but considerably off-centre on their larger EM2 cousins. *Transport Treasury.***

26022

Built Gorton 9/2/51.
To traffic: 20/9/51.
Works No.1025 *revised to* No.1029.

Renumbered: E26022 – ?/?
Renumbered: 76022 – 21/4/72.

Repairs:
Wath 28/6–12/7/52 **NC**;
Gorton 29/7–6/8/54 **CH** (40,930 miles);
Gorton 26/11–10/12/55 **CH** (99,704 miles);
Gorton 31/5–29/6/57 **CH** (169,566 miles);
Gorton 14/3–17/4/58 **CL** [cost £59] (201,127 miles);
Gorton 11/6–2/9/59 **HG** [cost £3,446] (252,350 miles);
Gorton 17–21/11/61 **NC** (95,007 miles);
Gorton <3/3/63>;
Crewe 30/4/70–24/8/70> **HG**, *AB, CC and MU fitted*;
Crewe <24/10/71–21/4/72 **CL** *accident damage*;
Withdrawn: July 1981.

With steam working the goods yard here, 26022 hauls a westbound mixed freight through a sunny Hazlehead on 19th June 1952. *Transport Treasury*.

26023

Built Gorton 14/2/51.
To traffic: 20/9/51.
Works No.1026 *revised to* No.1030.

Renumbered: E26023 – 12/66.
Renumbered: 76023 – 9/73.

Repairs:
Gorton 8/3–12/4/52 **CL** (4,894 miles);
Gorton 3–10/10/53 **CH** (40,040 miles);
Gorton 29/11–10/12/55 **CH** (120,049 miles);
Gorton 11/3–17/4/57 **NC** (191,556 miles);
Gorton 29/11–21/12/57 **CH** (208,777 miles);
Gorton 23/4–16/6/60 **HG** [cost £3,654] (317,032 miles);
Gorton 17/8/60 **NC** (6,147 miles);
Crewe <9/10–18/12/66;
Crewe 20/6–4/8/69> **HG**, *AB, CC and MU fitted*;
Doncaster <1/9/73>;
Crewe 5/12/75–?/?/76>;
Withdrawn: July 1981.

Passing 26025 and 26044 in the temporary stabling point siding, a semi-smartly turned out 26023 heads away from Penistone with a westbound passenger working on 26th June 1954. *J.W.Armstrong (ARPT).*

This illustration is undated but we can assume that 26023 had just arrived back at Gorton after completing its electrical equipment fitting out at Dukinfield. Therefore we can pin down the date to the early part of September 1951 – this Bo+Bo went into traffic on 20th September – when testing and last minute adjustments would be taken care of by Gorton's staff. Note the EM1 cab on the ground. ***K.H.Cockerill (ARPT).***

The accumulation of 'road dirt' is beginning to obliterate the last digits of the running numbers of both 26023 and 26045. Weekend rest, Wath depot, 1st May 1966. ***A.Ives (ARPT).***

26024

Built Gorton 1/3/51.
To traffic: 25/9/51.
Works No.1027 *revised to* No.1031.

Renumbered: E26024 – *by* 11/68.
Renumbered: 76024 – 11/73.

Repairs:
Gorton 11/6–27/9/52 **CL** (12,529 miles);
Gorton 13–23/1/54 **CH** (38,684 miles);
Gorton 15–19/2/55 **CH** (71,545 miles);
Gorton 30/7–31/8/57 **CH** (186,677 miles);
Gorton 9–26/3/59 **CH** [cost £1,195] (253,284 miles);
Gorton 22/2–28/4/60 **HG** [cost £4,161] (293,333 miles);
Gorton 4–8/11/61 **NC** (65,855 miles);
Crewe 13/12/68–15/4/69 **HG**, *AB, CC and MU fitted*;
Doncaster <7/10/73>;
Crewe <24/9/78>;
Withdrawn: July 1981.

With the aid of an unseen banker (*see* also page 37), 26024 ascends the grade at Worsborough with a westbound mineral working on Thursday 17th May 1956. *Transport Treasury*.

(top) **26024 sports lined green livery but no yellow warning panel at Wath on 7th October 1962. Sister 26018 and Brush Type 2 diesel D5824 are in attendance. Note that 26018 has the yellow panel.** ***Unknown photographer.***

(above) **21st March 1973, Guide Bridge: E26024 now has blue livery with full yellow ends and the double arrow motif/symbol, not to mention MU equipment.** ***Norman Preedy.***

(left) **76024 at Wath, circa 1977. Having acquired Timken roller bearing bogies, the EM1 will retain them to withdrawal.** ***Brian North.***

26025

Built Gorton 15/3/51.
To traffic: 4/1/52.
Works No.1032.

Renumbered: E26025 – 6/69.
Renumbered: 76025 – 8/72.

Repairs:
Gorton 8–14/2/53 **CL** (16,064 miles);
Gorton 13–19/8/54 **CH** *accident damage* (50,998 miles);
Gorton 30/7/56–19/1/57 HI (139,213 miles);
Gorton 2–11/12/58 **CH** [cost £1,215] (227,003 miles);
Gorton 25/8–3/9/59 **CL** [cost £389] (258,064 miles);
Gorton 25/11–4/12/59 **NC** (268,161 miles);
Gorton 3–8/6/60 **CH** [cost £ 1,408] (290,356 miles);
Gorton 26/8/60 **NC** (299,352 miles);
Crewe 18/9–20/12/64;
Crewe <19/2/67>;
Crewe <22/6/69> **HG**, *AB, CC and MU fitted*;
Crewe <24/10/71–6/8/72> **CL** *accident damage*;
Crewe <29/10/76–14/1/77> *(like 76032 [also in shops at this time] this engine carried Gorton 1039 works plates too!)*;
Withdrawn: July 1981.

With a slightly crumpled cab side sheet, 26025 gets on with 'ticking over' at Wath depot on 14th March 1953. This view of the north end of the shed at Wath affords us a look at the switch gear which enabled current to be shut off from the overhead inside the building. *Transport Treasury.*

26025 was another which had acquired a set of Timken axlebox equipped bogies by 1966 but had lost its lined green livery for the blue livery instead, courtesy of Crewe works. However, note that no yellow warning panel has been applied. The EM1 is stabled at Wath on Sunday 1st May 1966. *A.Ives (ARPT).*

Blue liveried 26025 resides near the traverser at Crewe works on an unknown date in the Sixties'. *Photographer Unknown.*

26026

Built Gorton 30/3/51.
To traffic: 4/1/52.
Works No.1033.

Renumbered: E26026 – *by* 7/69.
Renumbered: 76026 – 2/74.

Repairs:
Gorton 12–26/4/52 **CL** (6,174 miles);
Gorton 3–26/9/52 **CL** (14,409 miles);
Gorton 2–26/6/54 **CH** (42,336 miles);
Gorton 27/5–16/6/56 **CH** (129,075 miles);
Gorton 8/2–7/5/58 **CH** [cost £1,734] (207,404 miles);
Gorton 23/12/59–20/2/60 **HG** [cost £3,772] (281,638 miles);
Gorton 31/8/60 **NC** (20,660 miles);
Crewe <28/7/65>;
Crewe 25/7–2/8/69> **HG**, *AB, CC and MU fitted*;
Crewe <5/4/74–17/5/74>;
Withdrawn: July 1981.

With 26025 in tow, 26026 leads an eastbound mineral empties through Hazlehead on 19th June 1952 after commencement of the electric services west of Penistone to Dunford Bridge. *Transport Treasury*.

26026, reportedly at Wath depot with passenger stock! Both the date and event are unknown to this writer but during the 1950s British Railways usually ran special trains conveying politicians, local dignitaries and BR officials over new sections of railway and associated installations. This may well have been the 'press' special mentioned elsewhere in this tome and which was reputedly the first 'passenger' train to ascend Worsborough bank with electric haulage. *Authors coll.* *(below)* **76026 was undergoing some element of internal HT repair at Reddish on 2nd July 1978. The doorway halfway up the wall above the EM1 belonged to the pantograph repair shop and with its landing, was able to accept craned pantographs directly into the workshop for overhaul or repair. Immediately in front of the locomotive is one of the electric powered capstans used to move the locomotives around this shop. Of note is the cleanliness of the place which, with its pastel shades of off-white and blue gave it an air of modernity. *Hugh P.Searle.***

26027

Built Gorton 13/4/51.
To traffic: 24/1/52.
Works No.1034.

Renumbered: E26027 – 11/65.
Renumbered: 76027 – 1/74.

Repairs:
Gorton 9/2–7/3/52 **CL** (365 miles);
Gorton 25/7–20/9/52 **CL** (9,998 miles);
Gorton 16–23/10/54 **CL** (59,097 miles);
Gorton 25/9–3/11/56 **CH** (146,027 miles);
Gorton 1–4/2/58 **NC**;
Gorton 20/2–4/3/59 **CH** [cost £1,410] (249,353 miles);
Gorton 22/1–10/2/60 **CL** [cost £176] (284,226 miles);
Gorton 15/9–27/10/60 **HG** [cost £3,589] (310,390 miles);
Crewe <22/6/63>;
Crewe <7–14//11/65>;
Crewe 7/11–16/12/69> **HG**, *AB, CC and MU fitted*;
Crewe <19/5/74>;
Withdrawn: July 1981.

76027 waits for attention inside the servicing shed at Reddish on 19th March 1974. MU fitted, this example worked to the very end. To accommodate MU connections on the front of the cab the handrail has been bent upwards to clear the sockets. *Norman Preedy*.

26028

Built Gorton 26/4/51.
To traffic: 16/1/52.
Works No.1035.

Renumbered: E26028 – 2/66.
Renumbered: 76028 – 11/73.

Repairs:
Gorton 10–25/4/52 **CL** (5,228 miles);
Wath 14–21/6/52 **NC**;
Gorton 11–16/10/54 **CH** (61,259 miles);
Gorton 20/1–18/2/56 **CH** (114,545 miles);
Gorton 9/12/57–18/1/58 **CH** (199,723 miles);
Gorton 3/9–23/10/59 **HG** [cost £4,766] (272,653 miles);
Gorton 10–12/10/60 **NC** (41,041);
Crewe <1–5/5/64>
Crewe <30/1/66>; *Blue.*
Crewe <22/8–3/11/69 **HG**, *AB, CC and MU fitted*;
Doncaster <1/11/73>;
Withdrawn: July 1981.

(*above*) Any Sunday at Wath depot was a good time to photograph upwards of a dozen of the class stabled for their day-off. 1st May 1966 was no exception and 26028 shows off its corridor side to the camera. Note the Timken axleboxes. *A.Ives (ARPT).*

(*left*) Seven years later as E26028, the EM1 has blue livery, full yellow ends, BR crest and it has lost the Timken equipped bogies. It has however become one of the select band of MU fitted members of the class. Guide Bridge SP 21st March 1973; a fine, sunny day it will be noted. *Norman Preedy.*

26029

Built Gorton 7/5/51.
To traffic: 28/12/51.
Works No.1032 *revised to* 1036.

Renumbered: E26029 – 12/66.
Renumbered: 76029 – 2/74.

Repairs:
Gorton 11/6–25/7/52 **CL** (11,532 miles);
Gorton 10–17/10/53 **CH** (37,794 miles);
Gorton 21/10–5/11/55 **CH** (96,895 miles);
Gorton 12/10–9/11/57 **CH** (191,790 miles);
Gorton 6/10–27/11/59 **HG** [cost £3,832] (276,704 miles);
Gorton 7/9/60 **NC** (35,530 miles);
Crewe <1/11/64>;
Crewe <18/11–18/12/66;
Crewe 22/2/70–8/3/70> **HG**, *AB, CC and MU fitted*;
Crewe <21/6/74–12/8/74>;
Withdrawn: July 1981.

Yet to acquire the retro cut horizontal slots beneath the large ventilation grill (*see* Detail), 26029 runs through Penistone with an eastbound freight on 26th June 1954. Note the five new mineral wagons heading the train. *J.W.Armstrong (ARPT).*

(top) **Basking in the Yorkshire sunshine, 26029 is stabled at the south end of Wath depot on 17th July 1955.** ***K.R.Pirt.*** *(centre)* **26029 from another aspect on that Sunday at Wath in July 1955.** ***K.R.Pirt.*** *(above)* **26029 stands outside the north end of Wath shed on Sunday 31st May 1959. By now the once 'bright' horizontal handrail and front window frames are becoming tarnished. However, a Heavy General overhaul is but four months away.** ***A.R.Thompson (ARPT).***

26030

Built Gorton 24/5/51.
To traffic: 28/12/51.
Works No.1033 *revised to* 1037.
Renumbered: E26030 – 15/12/68.
Renumbered: 76030 – 12/72.

Repairs:
Gorton 28/4–7/5/52 **CL** (5,960 miles);
Gorton 12–29/7/54 **CH** (34,421 miles);
Gorton 2–20/11/54 **CL** (42,819 miles);
Gorton 12–15/1/55 **CL** (45,866 miles);
Gorton 11–24/11/56 **CH** (131,804 miles);
Gorton 23–30/10/58 **CH** [cost £1,421] (220,565 miles);
Gorton 13–28/1/60 **CL** [cost £109] (273,575 miles);
Gorton 2–7/5/60 **CL** (285,251 miles);
Gorton 29/8–14/10/60 **HG** [cost £3,046] (297,479 miles);
Gorton 23–30/11/60 **CH** (4,171 miles);
Gorton 17/7–4/8/61 **CL** (28,539 miles);
Crewe <9/10–1/11/64>;
Crewe ?/?/68–2/4/69> **HG**, *AB, CC and MU fitted*;
Doncaster <1/12/72>;
Withdrawn: July 1981.

26031

Built Gorton 6/6/51.
To traffic: 11/1/52.
Works No.1038.
Renumbered: E26031 – ?/?

Repairs:
Wath 5–12/7/52 **NC**;
Gorton 29/8–3/10/53 **CH** (39,383 miles);
Gorton 20/8–27/10/55 **CH** (105,042 miles);
Gorton 28/6–17/8/57 **CH** (193,436 miles);
Gorton 13–19/8/59 **CH** [cost £1,395] (290,349 miles);
Gorton 13–14/10/60 **NC** (338,929 miles);
Gorton 17/12/60–10/2/61 **HG** (347,780 miles);
Crewe <30/1–23/4/72> for c/u.
Withdrawn: October 1971 *after accident damage*.
Cut up at Crewe 1972.

26032

Built Gorton 28/6/51.
To traffic: 16/1/52.
Works No.1039.
Renumbered: E26032 – ?/?
Renumbered: 76032 – 1/72.

Repairs:
Gorton 29/8–19/9/53 **CH** (36,084 miles);
Gorton 12–20/8/55 **CL** (102,567 miles);
Gorton 24–28/7/56 **CL** (143,993 miles);
Gorton 20/1–1/3/58 **CH** [cost £1,314] (214,250 miles);
Gorton 3/11–24/12/59 **HG** [cost £3,079] (292,530 miles);
Gorton 7–15/10/60 **CL** (32,560 miles);
Gorton 7–10/1/61 **NC** (43,079 miles);
Crewe <17/10/65>;
Crewe <27/10–27/11/67>;
Crewe <29/10–12/12/76> **HG**, *AB, CC and MU fitted, VB removed 1/77.*
Withdrawn: July 1981.

26033

Built Gorton 28/6/51.
To traffic: 18/1/52.
Works No.1040.

Renumbered: E26033 – 5/67.
Renumbered: 76033 – 1/74.

Repairs:
Gorton 21/4–29/5/52 **CL** (6,379 miles);
Gorton 24/3–24/4/54 **CH** (49,432 miles);
Gorton 30/11–17/12/55 **CH** (114,896 miles);
Gorton 11–20/10/56 **CL** (154,715 miles);
Gorton 24/5–22/6/57 **CL** (181,736 miles);
Gorton 15/4–23/5/58 **CH** (221,380 miles);
Gorton 17/10–9/12/59 **HG** [cost £3,638] (283,604 miles);
Gorton 9–16/11/61 **NC** (80,932 miles);
Crewe <12/8/64>;
Crewe 17/2–21/5/67;
Crewe <8/11/70>;
Crewe <7/12/75–4/4/76> **HG**, *AB, CC and MU fitted, VB removed;*
Into Store: Reddish June 1980.
Re-instated: September 1980.
Withdrawn: July 1981.

26033 keeps a grip of its empty mineral train as it runs downhill through the rock cutting west of Penistone. Modellers note, there is a host of detail here. *Ron Hodge.*

26033 in blue and with full yellow ends but retaining the BR crest and still sans prefix. Godley Junction 21st March 1973. ***Norman Preedy.***

Now MU fitted and minus the vacuum brake facility, 76033 and an unidentified sister wait in the servicing shed at Reddish on 20th March 1977. 76033 is still wearing one of its workplates. Note the Permanent Way equipment behind the far locomotive. ***Hugh P.Searle.***

26034

Built Gorton 23/7/51.
To traffic: 18/1/52.
Works No.1041.

Renumbered: E26034 – 4/66.
Renumbered: 76034 – 10/73.

Repairs:
Gorton 21/4–17/5/52 **CL** (6,425 miles);
Gorton 5/7–20/9/52 **CL** (6,978 miles);
Gorton 30/8–7/9/54 **CH** (44,204 miles);
Gorton 3–27/11/54 **CL** (49,600 miles);
Gorton 7/1–26/2/55 **CH** (53,609 miles);
Gorton 11–14/5/55 **CL** (62,073 miles);
Gorton 1–25/5/57 **CH** (154,296 miles);
Gorton 27/4–4/8/59 **HG** [cost £3,180] (244,254 miles);
Gorton 25–30/11/61 **NC** (100,389 miles);
Crewe <3/5/64>;
Crewe <26/4/66; *Blue.*
Doncaster <7/10/73>;
Crewe <17/5/74–23/9/74>;
Crewe <24/11/74–3/2/75> **HG** *AB fitted.*
Crewe 2/4 – ?/8/76> *MU and CC fitted 8/76;*
Reddish 30/6/78 – ?/? **CL** *accident damage.*
Withdrawn: July 1981.

26034 presents the Crewe version of blue livery applied to the class. The EM1 is stabled at Wath on Mayday 1966, which in that particular year happened to be a Sunday. ***A.Ives (ARPT).***

26035

Built Gorton 1/8/51.
To traffic: 24/1/52.
Works No.1042.

Repairs:
Gorton 25/4–16/5/53 **CH** (33,831 miles);
Gorton 28/6–10/7/54 **CH** (55,198 miles);
Gorton 12–19/11/55 **CL** (111,341 miles);
Gorton 28/7–11/8/56 **CL** (141,985 miles);
Gorton 26/8–12/10/57 **CH** (193,366);
Gorton 2/5–30/6/60 **HG** [cost £3,960] (311,172), *green livery*;
Crewe <1/10/67>;
Withdrawn: March 1970 at Reddish as 26035.

(below) **Looking rather splendid, 26035 is in the process of receiving the last brush strokes of its lined Brunswick green livery in the works yard at Gorton in June 1960. Less than ten years afterwards it would be withdrawn and later cut up at Reddish depot. Its TOPS identity was eventually taken by sister 76018.** *(bottom)* **26035 from the other end after that Heavy General in 1960.** ***both Norman Preedy.***

26036

Built Gorton 14/8/51.
To traffic: 1/2/52.
Works No.1043.

Renumbered: E26036 – 1/66.
Renumbered: 76036 – 1/74.
Renumbered: 76003 – 10/76.

Repairs:
Gorton 20/3–24/4/54 **CH** (49,890 miles);
Gorton 29/12/55–14/1/56 **CH** (116,747 miles);
Gorton 18/10–23/11/57 **CH** (198,323 miles);
Gorton 15/4–9/5/58 **CL** (216,538 miles);
Gorton 4/4–26/5/60 **HG** [cost £3,525] (303,592 miles);
Gorton 19/8/60 **NC** (10,402 miles);
Crewe <14/6/64>;
Crewe <17/10/65>;
Crewe <30/1/66>;
Crewe <14/3/71>;
Crewe <10/76>.
Into Store: Reddish, August 1980 Ss.
Withdrawn: July 1981.

On Saturday 27th August 1955 No.26036 takes advantage of the servicing facility offered by the short-lived electric locomotive shed which had been erected at Darnall for this class. *Transport Treasury*.

26037

Built Gorton 31/8/51.
To traffic: 1/2/52.
Works No.1044.

Renumbered: E26037 – 9/10/66.
Renumbered: 76037 – 3/72.

Repairs:
Wath 14–21/6/52 **CL**;
Gorton 6/2–6/3/54 **CH** (54,698 miles);
Gorton 9–12/2/55 **CL** (86,634 miles);
Gorton 4/3–13/4/57 **CH** (180,296 miles);
Gorton 26/2–20/5/59 **HG** [cost £3,540] (268,716 miles);
Gorton 10–13/9/60 **NC** (56,147 miles);
Gorton 8–18/9/61 **CL** (100,913 miles);
Gorton 3–8/11/61 **CL** (105,905 miles);
Crewe 24/7–9/10/66;
Crewe <1/3/72>;
Crewe <1/76> **HG**, *AB, CC and MU fitted, VB removed;*
Crewe 29/10–12/12/76>;
Reddish <9/79> *bogie change*;
Withdrawn: October 1971.
Reinstated: November 1971.
Withdrawn: July 1981.

Besides sporting the BR crest, which was hardly discernible against the rail blue (in monochrome!), 76037 was still wearing the Condensed Grotesque style figures of the green era when it was photographed at Reddish on Wednesday 21st August 1974. Of course all that was to change at the next works visit when the BR double arrow symbol was applied and new Gill sans style numbers were put onto the cab side sheet on the driver's side only. Finally, it was fitted with multiple working gear, air brakes, and had the vacuum brake removed; not bad for a locomotive that was once on the brink. 76037 had been withdrawn in October 1971 only to be re-instated the following month; it went on to thrive and was amongst the last of the class still working when the end came in July 1981. ***Norman Preedy.***

26038

Built Gorton 13/9/51.
To traffic: 4/4/52.
Works No.1045.

Renumbered: E26038 – 6/65.
Renumbered: 76038 – 10/72.
Renumbered: 76050 – 10/76.

Repairs:
Gorton 7/6–7/7/54 **CH** (46,738 miles);
Gorton 2–7/5/55 **NC**;
Gorton 18/2–10/5/56 **CH** (116,803 miles);
Gorton 10–19/10/57 **CL** (171,836 miles);
Gorton 31/3–13/4/59 **CH** [cost £1,746] (232,339 miles);
Gorton 27–29/10/60 **NC** (299,167 miles);
Gorton 28/11/60–13/1/61 **HG** [cost £3,347] (302,843 miles);
Gorton 18–21/1/61 **NC** (54 miles);
Gorton <1/9/62>;
Crewe <16/5/65>;
Crewe 18/11/66–22/1/67>;
Crewe ?/12/68–27/1/69>;
Crewe <1/10/72>;
Crewe <3–12/12/76>;
Withdrawn: February 1977. *Stored at Reddish depot and removed from bogies by 1/4/78.*

76038 at Guide Bridge SP Wednesday on 21st August 1974, a couple of years before it became 76050! *Norman Preedy.*

26039

Built Gorton 24/9/51.
To traffic: 12/4/52.
Works No.1046.

Renumbered: E26039 – ?/?
Renumbered: 76039 – 3/74.
Renumbered: 76048 – 10/76.

Repairs:
Wath 5–12/7/52 **NC**;
Gorton 2–9/1/54 **CH** (42,448 miles);
Gorton 21/12/55–7/1/56 **CH** (111,512 miles);
Gorton 8/12/56–12/1/57 **CH** (153,997 miles);
Gorton 18/12/58–3/1/59 **CH** [cost £1,314] (243,469 miles);
Gorton 3–6/9/60 **NC** (319,208 miles);
Gorton 10/10–16/11/60 **HG** [cost £3,371] (323,468 miles);
Gorton <14/10/62>;
Crewe <19/9/65>;
Crewe <27/6/71>;
Withdrawn: February 1977.

Having been used as a 'taxi' in the time honoured tradition of footplatemen everywhere, 26039 stops at Guide Bridge station (Train Crew HQ west of Woodhead) to allow a couple of Motormen to dismount from the cab and onto the platform. En route to Reddish depot on an unrecorded date, the crew of the EM1 will have the evening sun to contend with throughout the less than ten minute journey. *K.R.Pirt.*

26040

Built Gorton 11/10/51.
To traffic: 21/4/52.
Works No.1047.

Renumbered: E26040 – *after* 9/69.
Renumbered: 76040 – 2/74.

Repairs:
Gorton 10/10/53–2/1/54 **CH** (39,269 miles);
Gorton 3–24/9/55 **CH** (96,522 miles);
Gorton 26/1–23/2/57 **CH** (159,566 miles);
Gorton 3/4–29/6/57 **CH** (164,821 miles);
Gorton 20–21/5/59 **CL** [cost £1,394] (250,546 miles);
Gorton 12/11–23/12/60 **HG** [cost £3,131] (312,941 miles);
Gorton <15/12/62>;
Crewe <28/7/65>;
Crewe <5/3/67>;
Crewe 25/9–8/11/70>;
Crewe <11/74>.
Into Store: August 1980 Ss.
Re-instated: November 1980.
Withdrawn: July 1981.

With just the front pantograph in contact - the front one note - 26040 runs through Penistone with eastbound mineral empties on Saturday 14th March 1953. This was of course during the period when the electric locomotives were working freight only over the section east of Woodhead tunnel as far as Wath. *Transport Treasury*.

Some nice roof detail is revealed by 26040 and an unidentified sister stabled at Orgreave in February 1958. ***W.R.E.Lewis (ARPT).***

Obviously not having to visit Crewe in recent years, 26040 retains its lined green livery in this 14th May 1967 illustration at Reddish depot. Flanked by two diesel-electric locomotives, left (Newton Heath's jack-shaft 0-6-0 shunter 12024) and rear (Sulzer Type 2), the EM1 is well used to 'foreign' diesel locomotives sharing the depot facilities. ***A.Ives (ARPT).***

An original condition EM1 at Wath, on the last day of May 1959! Black liveried 26040 has not yet had any 'holes' cut out of the bodywork at strategic locations but that operation will take place at its next HG in late 1960. *Unknown photographer*.

76040 was another of the class which survived to the end of MSW workings. On Wednesday 16th March 1977 it was stabled at Reddish depot awaiting attention from the staff. Evidence of bogie interchange is seen twice in this illustration: The two drilled holes on the lower section of the bufferbeam, to the right of the coupling, reveal that a heating connection was once fitted; the axle boxes are of the Timken roller bearing type. *Norman Preedy*.

26041

Built Gorton 25/10/51.
To traffic: 21/4/52.
Works No.1048.

Renumbered: E26041 – ?/?
Renumbered: 76041 – 3/74.

Repairs:
Wath 20–28/6/52 **CL**;
Gorton 2–16/1/54 **CH** (42,719 miles);
Gorton 4–22/10/55 **CH** (100,164 miles);
Gorton 16/5–8/6/57 **CH** (172,988 miles);
Gorton 13–25/4/59 **CH** [cost £1,284] (258,324 miles);
Gorton 28/4–1/5/59 **NC** (258,683 miles);
Gorton 19–20/9/60 **NC** (317,846 miles);
Gorton 2/11–13/12/60 **HG** [cost £3,131] (323,027 miles);
Gorton 17–24/3/61 **CL** [cost £49] (8,801 miles);
Crewe <24/4/65>;
Crewe 25/9–8/11/70>;
Crewe <12/74>.
Into Store: Reddish, 18th April 1980, Su.
Withdrawn: November 1980.

26041, with just one pantograph in contact, resided at the south end of Reddish depot on Sunday 3rd July 1966. ***A.Ives (ARPT).***

26042

Built Gorton 22/11/51.
To traffic: 19/5/52.
Works No.1049.

Repairs:
Gorton 2–16/1/54 **CL**;
Gorton 26/8–4/9/54 **NC**;
Gorton 13–16/9/54 **NC**;
Gorton 3–6/11/54 **CL** (14,539 miles);
Gorton 10–24/12/55 **CH** (67,815 miles);
Gorton 17/3–6/4/57 **CH** (130,534 miles);
Gorton 8/6–24/8/57 **CH** (138,986 miles);
Gorton 25/7–9/8/58 **CH** [cost £392] (184,610 miles);
Gorton 23–29/3/60 **CH** [cost £1,391] (257,259 miles);
Gorton 8–22/2/61 **CL** [cost £236] (295,590 miles);
Gorton 23/6–1/9/61 **HG** (310,609 miles);
Stored: Su at Reddish 1/5/68–3/70
Withdrawn: March 1970 at Reddish as 26042.
Cut up on site at Reddish by private contractor.

26042 lay derelict and cannibalised at Reddish in July 1969. The list of missing parts included the much sought-after sand box lids; axle box cover plates, screw coupling, windows various! It was never to run again and after withdrawal in March 1970, another period of dereliction saw the EM1 cut up on site in 1971 by West Midlands scrap dealer John Cashmore of Great Bridge. Sister 26035, immediately behind, followed exactly the same course as 26042. *Shaw Plan.*

26043

Built Gorton 29/11/51.
To traffic: 29/5/52.
Works No.1050.

Renumbered: E26043 – 2/66.
Renumbered: 76043 – 4/72.

Repairs:
Gorton 19/1–6/2/54 **CL** (1,810 miles);
Gorton 20/8–7/9/54 **NC**;
Gorton 2–5/11/54 **CL** (18,155 miles);
Gorton 16–24/3/56 **CH** (78,938 miles);
Gorton 21/1–9/2/57 **CH** (120,096 miles);
Gorton 27/8–3/9/58 **CH** [cost £947] (192,309 miles);
Gorton <24/4/60> **NC**;
Gorton 23/5–6/7/60 **HG** [cost £3,388] (268,653 miles);
Crewe <30/1/66>;
Crewe <4/2/68>;
Crewe <23/4/72>;
Doncaster <4/3–6/5/73>;
Doncaster <7/10/73>;
Into store: Reddish July 1977.
Withdrawn: June 1978. *Grounded (off bogies) 28/2/79.*

Just over a year before withdrawal, 76043 occupied the stub siding at the road entrance to Reddish depot on 30th March 1977. ***Norman Preedy.***

26044

Built Gorton 15/12/51.
To traffic: 11/6/52.
Works No.1051.

Renumbered: E26044 – 11/67.
Renumbered: 76044 – 3/72.
Renumbered: 76031 – 3/76.

Repairs:
Gorton 16–26/11/55 **CH** (76,380 miles);
Gorton 9/4–11/5/57 **CH** (141,217 miles);
Gorton 7/8–14/10/59 **HG** [cost £4,160] (241,921 miles);
Gorton 3–4/10/60 **NC** (43,249 miles);
Crewe <14–23/3/65>;
Crewe <26/11/67>;
Crewe <20/2–?/3/72>;
Crewe 18/9/75–?/3/76 **HG**, *AB fitted, VB removed and MU & CC fitted 3/76.*
Into Store: Reddish, 5th May 1980 Ss.
Re-instated: September 1980.
Withdrawn: July 1981.

So what was all the fuss about in Penistone on this Saturday 26th June 1954. It was the changeover point from steam to electric traction for westbound passenger workings (26044 is nearest the camera), and electric to steam motive power for eastbound workings between Penistone and Sheffield. As yet, the electrification to Sheffield was not quite complete and it would be 20th September before a through electrically hauled passenger service between Manchester and Sheffield was possible. So, in the meantime this scene, on the south, Down side of the station, was enacted daily at Penistone. *J.W.Armstrong (ARPT).*

(above) **Now employed for the day, 26044 takes a Down passenger working (187) out of Penistone on Saturday 26th June 1954.** ***J.W.Armstrong.***

(right) **The long shadows created by the evening sun on Sunday 10th April 1960 highlight 26044 outside the north end of Wath shed. The Pennine winter has been kind to the EM1's lined green livery since 26044 left Gorton works after a Heavy General overhaul in the previous October. Note that the two horizontal slots beneath the large ventilator grill have become standard by this time but the small square holes cut into the cabs above the side windows on each side have yet to become reality. Evidence of indiscriminate bogie changing is revealed by the two bolt holes on the right side of the lower edge of the bufferbeam; these once held the bracket for a train heating hose.** ***Photographer Unknown.***

(right) **76044 in its later guise as 76031 at Reddish depot! The date is 16th March 1977, some twelve months after the identity change which took place at Crewe when equipment for MU operation was fitted to 76044. Note that the worksplates are still in situ.** ***Norman Preedy.***

26045

Built Gorton 4/1/52.
To traffic: 26/6/52.
Works No.1052.

Renumbered: E26045 – 6/65.

Repairs:
Gorton 19–23/4/55 **CL** (50,448 miles);
Gorton 3–31/12/55 **CH** *collision damage* (83,509 miles);
Gorton 2/8–7/9/57 **CH** (159,948 miles);
Gorton 30/6–2/9/60 **HG** [cost £3,483] (286,169 miles);
Gorton <27/5/62>;
Crewe <27/6/65>;
Crewe <20/12/70>;
Stored: Reddish Ss 1/5/68–29/11/71
Withdrawn: 29th November 1971.
Sent to Crewe 17th March 1972.
Cut up at Crewe April 1972.

Although undated, this illustration of 26045 outside the erecting shop at Gorton gives some clues as to an approximate date. The EM1 is in lined green livery and with a newly applied yellow warning panel on the front. The bogies have both been given a new application of gloss black paint and the Timken axlebox covers also appear freshly painted. The general appearance of the body gives the impression that the paintwork has not been refreshed and still carries a small amount of workshop dust. Therefore, this dates the image to circa May 1962. Its last visit to shops prior to that date was for a Heavy General in 1960 when fresh paint would have been evident all over the bodywork. Also, the yellow panel would not have been put on at that 1960 overhaul. *Kevin Hudspith.*

26046

Built Gorton 16/1/52.
To traffic: 8/8/52.
Works No.1053.

Renumbered: E26046 – 7/65.
Renumbered: 76046 – 2/74.

Repairs:
Gorton 2/8–3/9/55 **CH** (62,415 miles);
Gorton 16/6–13/7/57 **CH** (146,803 miles);
Gorton 16/12/57–2/1/58 **NC**;
Gorton 28/12/58–30/1/59 **CL** [cost £622] (204,654 miles);
Gorton 30/4–2/5/59 **NC** (216,880 miles);
Gorton 14/9–11/11/59 **HG** [cost £3,774] (233,722 miles);
Gorton 12–29/1/60 **CL** [cost £374] (8,389 miles);
Gorton 18/8/60 **NC** (32,741 miles);
Crewe <28/7/65>;
Crewe <4/2/68>;
Doncaster <23/5–?/9/75.
Into Store: Reddish 1/5/68–?/?;
Re-instated: ?/?.
Into Store: July 1980 Ss, Su August.
Withdrawn: November 1980.

(below) **In primer undercoat, 26046 is stabled on the works siding adjacent to Gorton motive power depot in 1952. Awaiting entry to the paint shop, the EM1 has a crudely chalked version of its fleet number on the cab side. *K.H.Cockerill (ARPT).*** *(bottom)* **Weekend stabling for 26046 at the east end of the electric servicing shed yard at Darnall motive power depot on 26th August 1956. *F.W.Hampson (ARPT).***

Shortly after it was named ARCHIMEDES, and given its lined green livery, No.26046 sports the old pattern original axleboxes at Reddish depot in June 1959. However, through the bogie changes made at major overhauls (and at Reddish depot) some of those locomotives furnished from new with roller-bearing axle fitted bogies would sometimes end up running on bogies equipped with the original axleboxes; likewise earlier engines would also run on roller-bearing bogies. The bogie changes normally affected both bogies and there are no recorded instances of 'one-of-each' being employed beneath the same locomotive. Note the small painted square on the lower body above the nearest bogie. *Book Law coll.*

76046 was stored unserviceable in August 1980 and condemned in the following November. Just over twelve months beforehand, on 12th August 1979, the Bo+Bo was happily generating air in the stabling sidings on the west side of Reddish depot, with a Class 40 for company. Reddish depot was probably doing as much maintenance work on diesels as on the shrinking electric fleet by this time and it was diesel work which kept the depot open for a long time after the 76s had been finished off. *Norman Preedy.*

26047

Built Gorton 31/1/52.
To traffic: 22/8/52.
Works No.1054.

Renumbered: E26047 – ?/?
Renumbered: 76047 – 2/74.

Repairs:
Gorton 27/4–23/5/55 **CH** (51,321 miles);
Gorton 5–26/1/56 **CH** (77,999 miles);
Gorton 13/10–17/11/56 **CH** (111,032 miles);
Gorton 28/12/58–12/1/59 **CH** [cost £1,198] (211,239 miles);
Gorton 3–16/11/59 **CL** [cost £379] (248,203 miles);
Gorton 29/2–10/3/60 **CL** [cost £166] (263,358 miles);
Gorton 25/7–13/9/60 **HG** [cost £3,466] (280,064 miles);
Gorton 2–12/10/61 **CL** (46,018 miles);
Crewe <1–10/5/64>;
Crewe <19/9/65>;
Crewe <9/6/70>;
Crewe <15–20/9/74>.
Into Store: Reddish, September 1980 Su.
Withdrawn: November 1980.

On 7th October 1962 – a Sunday – 26047 DIOMEDES heads the line-up of stabled EM1s which greeted visitors to Wath depot at weekends. The lined green livery and nameplates have been a part of this EM1 for some two years by now. Note that just like 26000, the nameplate and BR crest on all the named EM1s were off-centre but whereas the MV plate was dead-centre. It will soon be time for 26047 to take its turn on the Manchester–Sheffield passenger services where its heating boiler will be put to the test during the coming winter which proved to be one of the coldest on record. ***Unknown photographer.***

26048

Built Gorton 18/2/52.
To traffic: 10/9/52.
Works No.1055.

Renumbered: E26048 – 8/68.
Renumbered: 76048 – 5/72.
Renumbered: 76039 – 10/76.

Repairs:
Gorton 9/3–2/4/55 **CH** (43,573 miles);
Gorton 9/5–1/6/57 **CL** (136,280 miles);
Gorton 15/9–14/10/58 **CH** [cost £1,818] (192,986 miles);
Gorton 4/2–30/3/60 **HG** [cost £3,719] (255,955 miles);
Gorton 16–29/7/60 **CL** [cost £168] (10,149 miles);
Gorton 6–17/8/60 **NC** *Rectify* (10,274 miles);
Gorton 6–10/10/61 **CH** (59,946 miles);
Gorton <3/3/63>;
Crewe <12/5/63>;
Crewe <1–10/5/64>;
Crewe <7/5/68;
Crewe <16/12/68;
Crewe <5/1/77;
Crewe <24/9/77–9/12/77 **HG**, *AB, CC and MU fitted, VB removed 10/77 (dA);*
Reddish <20/5/78> *bogie change;*
Into Store: Reddish, September 1980.
Withdrawn: July 1981.

76048 loitering at Guide Bridge on 21st August 1974! Rebuilding to MU standard saw this Bo+Bo renumbered to 76039 in October 1976 but the actual rebuildinging did not start until the following October. *Norman Preedy*.

26049

Built Gorton 3/3/52.
To traffic: 27/9/52.
Works No.1056.

Renumbered: E26049 – ?/?
Renumbered: 76049 – 8/72.

Repairs:
Gorton 16/6–30/7/55 **CH** (54,899 miles);
Gorton 4–19/11/55 **CL** (66,728 miles);
Gorton 29/2–10/3/56 **CL** (79,569 miles);
Gorton 26–28/7/56 **CL** (95,790 miles);
Gorton 2–26/1/57 **CL** (114,848 miles);
Gorton 2–19/6/58 **CH** [cost £1,848] (177,832 miles);
Gorton 30/6–7/7/58 *Adjustment* (178,476 miles);
Gorton 11–12/2/59 **NC** *Weigh* (205,485 miles);
Gorton 27/2–26/3/59 **CL** [cost £337] (207,216 miles);
Gorton 16/6–23/8/60 **HG** [cost £3,345] (262,147 miles);
Gorton 5/10–9/11/61 **CL** (44,169 miles);
Gorton <14/10/62>;
Gorton <15/12/62>;
Gorton <3/3/63>;
Crewe <30/8–22/9/64>;
Crewe <1–17/11/64>;
Crewe <21/2/65>;
Crewe ?/12/69–25/8/70;
Crewe 21/4–6/8/72>;
Doncaster <4/75>.
Into Store: Reddish, August 1980 Ss, Su August.
Withdrawn: November 1980.

76049 shows all the signs of a hurried renumbering (August 1972) whereby the 7 replaced the 2 and the E was painted out multiplied by four! This is Reddish depot on Wednesday 21st March 1973 when the EM1 still had another seven years of service in front of it. Note those eyebrows! Behind is E26041 which was not renumbered until March 1974. *Norman Preedy.*

26050

Built Gorton 27/3/52.
To traffic: 19/11/52.
Works No.1057.

Renumbered: E26050 – 1/67.
Renumbered: 76050 – 11/71 *first of class.*
Renumbered: 76038 – 11/76 *last of class.*

Repairs:
Gorton 26/1–6/2/54 **CL** (0 miles);
Gorton 12–31/3/56 **CH** (85,382 miles);
Gorton 2/12/57–11/1/58 **CH** (157,286 miles);
Gorton 28/7–1/8/58 **NC** (180,943 miles);
Gorton 3/6–8/8/60 **HG** [cost £3,975] (265,59 miles); *Green livery + name.*
Gorton <15/12/62>;
Crewe <18/11/66–22/1/67;
Doncaster <11/71>;
Crewe <29/10/76–14/1/77>;
Crewe <14/5–3/6/77> **HG**, *AB, CC and MU fitted, VB removed 6/77 (dA).*
Into Store: Reddish June 1980 Ss.
Re-instated: September 1980.
Withdrawn: July 1981.

26050 was named STENTOR in August 1960. In order to place the BR crest above the new nameplate, Gorton created a flat plate to be fitted over the central body seam which was somewhat proud of the body sides and would have distorted the transfer. The crest used for this was smaller than the usual size applied to the unnamed members of the class. The date is 8th February 1964 and the Bo+Bo had just arrived at Sheffield (Victoria) with the 2.10 p.m. from Manchester (Piccadilly). The bodywork appears a bit shabby but it would be more than two years before the EM1 made a visit to Crewe for overhaul. *W.B.Yeadon.*

(right) **E26050 STENTOR heads a Manchester (Piccadilly)–Sheffield (Victoria) express circa 1968. Note that the BR crest, applied by Crewe at its last overhaul (finished 22nd January 1967) is one of the large variety and was obviously too big to fit on the plate specially fitted, by Gorton works, above the nameplate. *R.McAvoy*.**

(below) **With its train heating boiler working to maximum capacity, E26050 in blue (and road dirt grey) livery, heads west out of Penistone on 3rd January 1970. Note the position of the large size BR crest. *Unknown photographer*.**

(right) **Stabled at Guide Bridge on 22nd March 1973, 76050 was the first of the class to be given its TOPS number, an event which took place in November 1971. Not satisfied with that little nugget of '76' history under its belt, 76050 was renumbered yet again to 76038 in November 1976. In doing so, this locomotive then became the first and last of the class to be renumbered! Of course the second renumbering took place when 26050/76050/76038 was fitted for multiple unit working and it was deemed prudent to tidy up the relevant 'types' into numerical batches. *Norman Preedy*.**

26051

Built Gorton 5/5/52.
To traffic: 18/12/52.
Works No.1058.

Renumbered: E26051 *by* 8/4/69.
Renumbered: 76051 – 2/74.

Repairs:
Gorton 12–24/2/54 **CL** (0 miles);
Gorton 26/8–10/9/55 **H** (56,033 miles);
Gorton 22/5–9/6/56 **NC**;
Gorton 23/11–28/12/57 **CH** (159,330 miles);
Gorton 10–18/11/58 **CL** [cost £501] (202,343 miles);
Gorton 6–23/6/59 **CH** [cost £1,507] (229,570 miles);
Gorton 5–6/10/60 **NC** (292,414 miles);
Gorton 5/5–26/6/61 **HG** (376,836 miles);
Crewe <26/1/64>;
Crewe <20/12/70>;
Into Store: Reddish June 1980 Ss.
Re-instated: August 1980.
Withdrawn: July 1981.

26051 has just arrived at Penistone with an express from Manchester on Saturday 26th June 1954, and is about to uncouple so that a Darnall B1 4-6-0 can take the train on to Sheffield. This period during Penistone's railway history was perhaps the most intensive ever experienced but it wasn't to last much longer as all the changeovers from late September would be carried out in Sheffield. Note the pantographs are stretched virtually to their limit. Today, an hourly d.m.u. service between Sheffield and Huddersfield, via Barnsley, is the only railway activity which 'shatters' the peace of what is now a rather sleepy junction. The side of the station in view is long bereft of track, canopies and platforms although some of the station buildings survive in private business use. The Huddersfield Down line platform canopy can just be seen on the extreme right of the illustration. ***J.W.Armstrong (ARPT).***

(above) **In charge of an Up express, 26051 exits Woodhead tunnel and runs into the short cutting at Dunford Bridge on 26th June 1954. Over the top of the rise can be seen the cutting serving the old tunnels.** ***J.W.Armstrong (ARPT).***

(right) **Wondering when the next passenger working is due perhaps! 76051 waited in anticipation of the impossible at Reddish on 18th April 1981.** ***S.Carter.***

26052

Built Gorton 15/5/52.
To traffic: 31/1/53.
Works No.1059.

Renumbered: E26052 – 8/64.
Renumbered: 76052 – 2/74.

Repairs:
Gorton 6–13/3/54 **CL** (0 miles);
Gorton 27/11–14/12/54 **NC**;
Gorton 11–13/10/56 **CL** (102,861 miles);
Gorton 11/2–29/3/58 **CH** [cost £1,435] (170,228 miles);
Gorton 23–24/4/58 **NC** (173,465 miles);
Gorton 2–9/12/58 **CH** [cost £492] (203,380 miles);
Gorton 6–21/1/59 **CL** [cost £55] (207,399 miles);
Gorton 26/6–10/7/59 **CL** [cost £469] (229,322 miles);
Gorton 22–30/10/59 **CH** [cost 1,686] (241,231 miles);
Gorton 2–23/12/59 *Adjustment* (244,866 miles);
Gorton 22/8/60 **NC** (275,893 miles);
Gorton 10/6–18/8/61 **HG** (309,887 miles);
Crewe <12/8/64>;
Crewe <11/12/66>;
Into store: Reddish, July 1977.
Withdrawn: June 1978.

Languishing in the sidings located at the west side of the shed at Reddish, 76052 had been stripped of various parts when this scene was recorded on 20th May 1979. It had been stored unserviceable in July 1977 and condemned the following year. The roller bearing axlebox bogies fitted to 26052 when new had been exchanged by 1956 and for many years 26052 ran with the original bearing bogies fitted to the majority of the class but at some unrecorded date in later life 26052 regained the roller bearing bogies which it is fitted to in this illustration. *Norman Preedy.*

26053

Built Gorton 3/6/52.
To traffic: 11/3/53.
Works No.1060.

Renumbered: E26053 – 10/67.
Renumbered: 76053 – 3/74.

Repairs:
Gorton 4–20/3/54 **CL** (0 miles);
Gorton 21/4–5/5/56 **CH** (79,394 miles);
Gorton 23/6–4/8/56 **CH** (84,559 miles);
Gorton 2/8–5/9/58 **CL** [cost £2,138] (178,139 miles);
Gorton 23–29/9/58 **CL** [cost £88] (179,495 miles);
Gorton 29/12/59–7/1/60 **CL** [cost £386] (242,523 miles);
Gorton 18/8–6/10/60 **HG** [cost £3,299] (269,187 miles);
Gorton 18–25/8/61 **CL** (40,348 miles);
Gorton 6–17/10/61 **CH** (44,486 miles);
Crewe <2/1/66>;
Crewe <1–31/10/67> **CL** *accident damage*;
Crewe 13/6–29/9/70>;
Crewe 21/6–23/9/74>;
Reddish <10/76> *Boiler removed.*
Into Store: Reddish, June 1980 Ss.
Re-instated: September 1980.
Withdrawn: November 1980.

With a somewhat easy load of five bogies, 26053 coasts ‘down the bank’ at Torside in May 1955 with a Manchester service. The Bo+Bo is not looking its best on this date but then none of the class looked clean after a few weeks running in the so-called ‘mixed traffic’ black livery. *Norman Preedy*.

Ready with the express disc headcode on Saturday 18th June 1955, 26053 waits at Manchester (London Road) for the next arrival from Sheffield which it will work back to south Yorkshire. Note the newly acquired pair of slots cut into the bodywork just below the large ventilator. One of the original Timken batch, 26053 has managed to keep them up to this date. *F.W.Hampson (ARPT).* *(below)* **76053 stables outside the south end of the maintenance shop at Reddish on Sunday 27th April 1980. By this date the depot at Reddish was wholly responsible for looking after the EM1s and went to great lengths to keep the remaining members of the class in traffic. Occasionally a fresh coat of paint was applied but extreme measures, mainly cannibalisation, were 'practiced' in order to 'keep the flag flying'. 76053 did not last until the very end and was withdrawn during November, some of its parts therefore keeping others on the road. *Norman Preedy.***

26054

Built Gorton 4/7/52.
To traffic: 23/4/53.
Works No.1061.

Renumbered: E26054 – 21/5/67.
Renumbered: 76054 – 12/73.

Repairs:
Gorton 10–17/3/56 **CL** (77,289 miles);
Gorton 18/11–15/12/56 **CH** (108,221 miles);
Gorton 31/12/58–28/1/59 **CH** [cost £1,148] (205,034 miles);
Gorton 22/9–1/10/59 **CL** [cost £493] (234,039 miles);
Gorton 30/8/60 **NC** (276,839 miles);
Gorton <8/4/61>;
Crewe <14/3/65>;
Crewe 5/3–21/5/67;
Crewe ?/5–27/7/69;
Doncaster <12/73>.
Into store: Reddish, July 1977.
Re-instated: March 1978.
Into store: Reddish, July 1980 Ss.
Re-instated: September 1980.
Withdrawn: July 1981, *last of class*.

Brand new 26054 outside Gorton works in April 1953. The EM1 has been quarantined on one of the old coaling stage roads with chocks under each wheel and old sleepers placed across the track at each end of the locomotive. It is probable that adjustments to the handbrake were being undertaken. Whereas 26000 had ventilation louvers only on the corridor side of the machinery compartment, the production batch had them on both sides of the body. Barely discernible in this monochrome image, thin red lining has been applied just inside each of the body panels besides the cab side and front panels. A windscreen wiper has yet to be fitted to the driver's window, whilst a single horn resides on the cab roof. Note the Timken roller bearing axleboxes fitted to this later built example. *Authors coll.*

(top) **In 1966 the fleet numbers of the EM1 and EM2 locomotives began to be prefixed with the letter E and E26054 PLUTO, still in lined green livery, shows off its new identity at Manchester Piccadilly whilst heading the 4.10 p.m. to Sheffield on Saturday 18th May 1968. *R.McAvoy*.** *(above)* **E26054 offers a nice broadside view to the camera at Guide Bridge on 21st March 1973. Note that only one pantograph is raised and also that compared with the situation at Penistone for instance it is not just reflexed into contact. *Norman Preedy*.** *(below, left)* **Works plate No.1061 and prefixed number. Manchester Piccadilly 3rd January 1970. *Unknown photographer*.** *(below, right)* **Looking rather weathered, and tired, the PLUTO nameplate and British Rail double-arrow motif on 26054 at Manchester Piccadilly 3rd January 1970.**

26055

Built Gorton 6/8/52.
To traffic: 6/6/53.
Works No.1062.

Renumbered: E26055 – 9/66.
Renumbered: 76055 – 2/74.

Repairs:
Gorton 28/6–2/7/55 **CL** (43,822 miles);
Gorton 16/12/56–19/1/57 **CH** (114,476 miles);
Gorton 4/5–8/6/59 **CH** [cost £2,136] (217,641 miles);
Gorton 17–20/2/60 **CL** [cost £446] (247,861 miles);
Gorton 17/10/60 **NC** (276,748 miles);
Gorton 30/1–24/3/61 **HG** [cost £3,233] (290,417 miles);
Gorton 28/5–19/6/61 **CH** (7,100 miles);
Crewe <11/9/66>;
Crewe <14/3/71>;
Crewe <22/2/74>;
Withdrawn: February 1977.

(below) **Keeping a grip on things, boiler-fitted 26055 lends a hand shifting some of the heavy coal traffic westwards through Torside in May 1955. It was concluded as early as 1954 that the EM1 was more suited to working goods trains than passenger trains. Although the haulage capability of the class in passenger service was totally adequate, the riding qualities of the locomotives over 50 m.p.h. were far from ideal. *Norman Preedy*.**
(bottom) **On Sunday 16th October 1955, outside the shed at Sheffield Darnall, 26055 displays the remnants of silver paint on its buffer heads which was applied for reasons unknown.**

Although undated, this illustration was probably recorded in the summer of 1961 when 26055 had just completed a Casual Heavy repair where its original Timken Roller Bearing bogies were exchanged for these examples from the earlier-built batch of EM1s. It was only in the previous March that the Bo+Bo had completed a Heavy General overhaul so something drastic must have happened – to one or both bogies – shortly after the time it was released to traffic on 24th March, to have brought 26055 back to works at the end of May. It had covered just over 7,000 miles in traffic during those two months. ***Transport Treasury.***

Already withdrawn when this image was recorded at Reddish on Wednesday 30th March 1977, 76055, in company with similarly disposed 76057, is largely intact except for its plates. 76057 on the other hand managed to keep hold of a works plate at least. ***Norman Preedy.***

26056

Built Gorton 28/8/52.
To traffic: 19/7/53.
Works No.1063.

Renumbered: E26056 – 10/65.
Renumbered: 76056 – 2/74.

Repairs:
Gorton 9–6/9/54 **NC**;
Gorton 15/4–19/5/56 **CH** (83,097 miles);
Gorton 30/5–9/6/56 **CL** (86,173 miles);
Gorton 14/8–5/10/57 **CH** (140,678 miles);
Gorton 26/5–1/7/59 **CH** [cost £1,731] (228,291 miles);
Gorton 12–27/10/59 **CL** [cost £441] (240,643 miles);
Gorton 24–25/8/60 **NC** (277,678 miles);
Gorton 29/3–8/6/61 **HG** (303,200 miles);
Crewe <16/12/63;
Crewe <17/10/65>;
Crewe <22/1/67>;
Crewe 21/8/70–16/3/71;
Doncaster <1/2/74>;
Crewe 18/9/75>;
Withdrawn: June 1978.

(right) **A close-up of 26056's nameplate on 20th December 1969. Can you see the fixings? Nobody could unless you went inside the body of the EM1 where the relevant screws/bolts were safely located.** ***Transport Treasury.***

26056 TRITON enters Sheffield (Victoria) 28th August 1963 with a loaded iron ore train which originated in Birkenhead docks and was destined for Scunthorpe. Although this EM1 was equipped with a heating boiler from new, the train pipe connection had been removed at this date; the disconnected boiler was finally removed in November 1970. The square cut holes above the cab side windows were a retro-fitted form of ventilation which first started to appear in the 1960s. ***A.Ives (ARPT).***

Now wearing the E prefix and a change of numbering style, E26056 runs through Guide Bridge on 21st March 1973. ***Norman Preedy.***

76056 was never fitted out for multiple-unit working and kept its vacuum brake to the end. However, the EM1 did not itself last until the end of the class and was stored unserviceable in March 1978 only to be condemned three months later. On Tuesday 19th March 1974, 76056 was resting at Guide Bridge stabling point and is representative of the final livery borne by the class. Originally fitted with a heating boiler, that appliance was removed in November 1970 after the cessation of passenger services. ***Norman Preedy.***

26057

Built Gorton 26/9/52.
To traffic: 26/8/53.
Works No.1064.

Renumbered: E26057 – 10/66.
Renumbered: 76057 – 7/72.

Repairs:
Gorton 6–25/9/54 **NC**;
Gorton 15–28/1/56 **CH** (69,606 miles);
Gorton 25/8–1/9/56 **CL** (94,735 miles);
Gorton 8/3–16/5/58 **CH** [cost £2,065] (164,874 miles);
Gorton 11/2–11/4/60 **HG** [cost £3,869] (251,315 miles);
Gorton 19–22/4/60 **CL** (720 miles);
Gorton 26/7–6/8/60 **CL** [cost £179] (12,436 miles);
Crewe <12/8–12/10/64>;
Crewe <9/10/66>;
Crewe <9/6/68>;
Crewe 9/6/72>;
Reddish <10/76> *Boiler removed.*
Withdrawn: February 1977.

With the winter cold now behind it, 26057 ULYSSES is able to give its services to whoever requires them. On 8th May 1960 the rather smart Bo+Bo is stabled outside Wath shed with sister 26007 which has yet to be given the lined green livery afforded the class. 26057's immaculate appearance stems from a Heavy General overhaul completed on 11th April last when it was also named but note that the Timken axlebox bogies have been replaced with the standard axle box bogies. *Unknown photographer.*

Except for the asbestos, 76057's hulk would have perhaps made a nice cricket pavilion, scout hut, pigeon loft, (non)mobile home, allotment hut, restaurant, EM1, 76, ... Reddish 18th April 1981. *S.Carter.*

Mileages & Days Out Of Service

Data concerning mileages has been scant in some cases, prolific in others, and positively non-existant for most years. What has been available is presented here in five different tables, which cover the period from the late 1950s to the early 1960s. Hopefully the information will help the reader to understand what these locomotives were capable of and which ones were the stars, and which ones the damp squids. The information has been gleaned from the archives at Kew, York, and the History and Record cards. Accuracy has been the key but if any reader spots any differences with data in their own custody, this writer would like to hear from them via the usual channels.

It must be summer! A non-boiler fitted EM1 is getting some mileage in working a westbound passenger train at Penistone on Saturday 26th June 1954. No.26011 is the Bo+Bo in charge of what appear to be a rather interesting rake of vehicles. It was during these early duties that the unsuitability of the class for high-speed running was confirmed. *J.W.Armstrong (ARPT).*

It was unusual to see the EM2s running light engine east of Guide Bridge, but on a 12th May 1956, No.27000 proceeds east through Penistone. Initially it was envisaged that only the rear pantograph was to beused but dirty contact wires and wintry conditions over the Woodhead route, with ice on the wires, made it necessary to use both pantographs together on both classes. A consistent performer, 27000 clocked up the highest EM2 mileage in 1960. *J.W.Armstrong (ARPT).*

ACCUMULATIVE INDIVIDUAL MILEAGES as at 31st December 1957 CLASS EM1 and EM2

26000 @ 31/12/57 = 39906
26001 @ 31/12/57 = 151212
26002 @ 31/12/57 = 195226
26003 @ 31/12/57 = 166627
26004 @ 31/12/57 = 143103
26005 @ 31/12/57 = 161432
26006 @ 31/12/57 = 149989
26007 @ 31/12/57 = 165827
26008 @ 31/12/57 = 134081
26009 @ 31/12/57 = 167239
26010 @ 31/12/57 = 161264
26011 @ 31/12/57 = 197573
26012 @ 31/12/57 = 211070
26013 @ 31/12/57 = 204269
26014 @ 31/12/57 = 211512
26015 @ 31/12/57 = 216838
26016 @ 31/12/57 = 213731
26017 @ 31/12/57 = 198123
26018 @ 31/12/57 = 215198
26019 @ 31/12/57 = 177454
26020 @ 31/12/57 = 165059
26021 @ 31/12/57 = 200286
26022 @ 31/12/57 = 191600
26023 @ 31/12/57 = 210466
26024 @ 31/12/57 = 199329
26025 @ 31/12/57 = 185528
26026 @ 31/12/57 = 202655
26027 @ 31/12/57 = 198422
26028 @ 31/12/57 = 199723
26029 @ 31/12/57 = 197359
26030 @ 31/12/57 = 183865
26031 @ 31/12/57 = 212759
26032 @ 31/12/57 = 213180
26033 @ 31/12/57 = 207169
26034 @ 31/12/57 = 182705
26035 @ 31/12/57 = 203574
26036 @ 31/12/57 = 203703
26037 @ 31/12/57 = 214186
26038 @ 31/12/57 = 179683
26039 @ 31/12/57 = 198615
26040 @ 31/12/57 = 188069
26041 @ 31/12/57 = 200565
26042 @ 31/12/57 = 157845
26043 @ 31/12/57 = 161594
26044 @ 31/12/57 = 171459
26045 @ 31/12/57 = 175242
26046 @ 31/12/57 = 161708
26047 @ 31/12/57 = 162058
26048 @ 31/12/57 = 162260
26049 @ 31/12/57 = 156754
26050 @ 31/12/57 = 157286
26051 @ 31/12/57 = 159587
26052 @ 31/12/57 = 163715
26053 @ 31/12/57 = 149836
26054 @ 31/12/57 = 154868
26055 @ 31/12/57 = 153341
26056 @ 31/12/57 = 152053
26057 @ 31/12/57 = 158358

27000 @ 31/12/57 = 246541
27001 @ 31/12/57 = 261271
27002 @ 31/12/57 = 232029
27003 @ 31/12/57 = 233114
27004 @ 31/12/57 = 229900
27005 @ 31/12/57 = 235974
27006 @ 31/12/57 = 220526

INDIVIDUAL ANNUAL MILEAGES:

Loco.	1957	1958	1959	1960	1961
26000	-	16283	36054	35781	24894
26001	-	44780	44600	44132	35534
26002	-	34082	36293	37089	41291
26003	-	44297	41115	37573	44212
26004	-	42193	46873	37160	41832
26005	-	42498	47015	45354	31437
26006	-	46810	44351	46968	30969
26007	-	40998	48046	42876	33928
26008	-	39916	45455	45443	37341
26009	-	45152	43766	38415	41642
26010	-	45562	39857	38482	41794
26011	-	45194	45049	43881	33285
26012	-	48033	47104	37844	42536
26013	-	43422	34708	45494	41711
26014	-	43697	34891	42991	41745
26015	-	28616	46341	42652	43116
26016	-	40710	40612	40729	44217
26017	-	43785	45729	41644	34435
26018	-	42847	42192	39453	40195
26019	-	39814	45882	43600	38918
26020	-	46868	36519	46808	42067
26021	-	46383	32163	44147	41151
26022	-	39610	34343	43874	41130
26023	-	45829	46287	37314	39577
26024	-	44611	42498	37484	40768
26025	46315	43396	42238	42693	40432
26026	-	33555	45428	35999	42689
26027	-	44167	39812	36424	45421
26028	-	41339	37507	45014	41738
26029	-	45847	37776	43112	43926
26030	-	43983	44537	32853	36690
26031	-	47495	45752	41774	34952
26032	-	39388	40232	42338	43176
26033	-	39737	38411	44934	39320
26034	-	45840	33130	45139	41331
26035	-	46649	45042	38530	42780
26036	-	41710	46104	39318	42245
26037	-	46981	34955	43012	42336
26038	-	41143	43228	38801	40193
26039	-	44854	46057	39724	42065
26040	-	44025	44916	35983	41714
26041	-	45211	42421	35408	37219
26042	-	44911	44459	43706	33420
26043	-	44631	45356	37797	39195
26044	-	44654	34471	45422	43460
26045	-	43607	46065	36975	40527
26046	-	42860	34780	41394	43237
26047	-	49071	43727	38779	41726
26048	-	40209	48024	32154	42488
26049	-	41839	43414	34985	34841
26050	-	41925	47691	37346	40376
26051	-	48106	46765	48094	35994
26052	-	42078	40065	46744	34298
26053	-	42718	49969	37437	43036
26054	-	50125	42258	44271	36054
26055	-	46771	42265	43836	32435
26056	-	54454	43018	43037	35997
26057	-	38490	49323	37364	45588
27000	-	66876	76972	82961	74468
27001	-	67783	75340	63720	58073
27002	-	70536	63617	68045	64201
27003	-	66651	85509	66776	74496
27004	-	68640	74543	48801	76811
27005	-	56505	80644	62321	79041
27006	-	67850	69362	76000	73330

Mileage to first Heavy General - HG - overhaul (or Heavy Intermediate - HI):

Loco.	Date	Miles
26000	8/9/60	116042 (NC no data after 8/9/60)
26001	22/7/61	308644
26002	15/10/58	229417
26003	22/3/60	262513
26004	18/1/60	234079
26005	14/9/61	325748
26006	9/1/61	289143
26007	10/8/61	322988
26008	23/5/61	283219
26009	8/8/60	282611
26010	27/9/60	279444
26011	23/1/61	334415
26012	19/10/60	342867
26013	29/1/59	251666
26014	7/4/59	267844
26015	5/8/58	245301
26016	21/11/59	295053
26017	31/8/60	314985 (NC no data after 3/9/60)
26018	25/11/59	300188
26019	8/12/60	306750
26020	24/6/59	235753
26021	31/12/58	246849
26022	11/6/59	252350
26023	23/4/60	317032
26024	9/3/59	253284
26025	18/8/56	139213 (HI)
26026	22/12/59	281638
26027	15/9/60	310390
26028	3/9/59	272653
26029	6/10/59	276704
26030	29/8/60	297479
26031	17/12/60	347780
26032	3/11/59	292530
26033	17/10/59	283604
26034	27/4/59	244254
26035	2/5/60	311172
26036	4/4/60	303592
26037	26/2/59	268716
26038	28/11/60	302843
26039	10/10/60	323468
26040	12/11/60	312941
26041	2/11/60	323027
26042	23/6/61	310609
26043	23/5/60	268653
26044	7/8/59	241921
26045	30/6/60	286169
26046	14/9/59	233722
26047	25/7/60	280064
26048	4/2/60	255955
26049	16/6/60	262147
26050	3/6/60	265594
26051	5/5/61	376836
26052	10/6/61	309887
26053	18/8/60	269187
26054	30/8/60	276839 (NC no data after 30/8/60)
26055	30/1/61	290417
26056	29/3/61	303200
26057	11/2/60	251315
27000	28/4/61	501317 (CH no data after 8/6/61)
27001	26/10/61	518294 (CH no data after 19/12/61)
27002	10/11/61	486070 (NC no data after 10/11/61)
27003	18/10/61	513053 (CL no data after 25/10/61)
27004	3/10/60	414047 (CL no data after 26/11/60)
27005	25/10/60	421758 (CL no data after 3/11/60)
27006	14/9/61	488081 (CL no data after 26/9/61)

1963 MILEAGES EM1 and EM2 classes:

Twelve 'Week Ending' mileage periods on a monthly basis:
(a) Class; (b) Number used.; (c) Total miles worked (weekdays);
(d) Miles per weekday per unit (in use).

Week ending 23rd February:

(a)	(b)	(c)	(d)
EM1	51.6	46261	149.4
EM2	3.3	5289	267.1

Week ending 23rd March:

(a)	(b)	(c)	(d)
EM1	49.8	47235	158.1
EM2	4.0	6365	265.2

Week ending 6th April:

(a)	(b)	(c)	(d)
EM1	52.2	46307	147.9
EM2	3.7	5334	240.3

Week ending 18th May:

(a)	(b)	(c)	(d)
EM1	51.3	44266	143.8
EM2	5.2	7348	235.5

Week ending 15th June:

(a)	(b)	(c)	(d)
EM1	52.1	41358	132.3
EM2	4.7	7484	265.4

Week ending 13th July:

(a)	(b)	(c)	(d)
EM1	50.4	40992	135.6
EM2	5.0	7091	236.4

Week ending 3rd August:

(a)	(b)	(c)	(d)
EM1	53.2	38300	120.0
EM2	4.7	6782	240.5

Week ending 7th September:

(a)	(b)	(c)	(d)
EM1	51.2	42927	139.7
EM2	5.0	7119	237.3

Week ending 5th October:

(a)	(b)	(c)	(d)
EM1	51.0	43461	142.0
EM2	5.3	6795	213.7

Week ending 2nd November:

(a)	(b)	(c)	(d)
EM1	52.0	46419	148.8
EM2	4.4	7320	277.3

Week ending 30th November:

(a)	(b)	(c)	(d)
EM1	51.3	43246	140.5
EM2	4.8	8252	286.5

Week ending 21st December:

(a)	(b)	(c)	(d)
EM1	51.3	46589	151.4
EM2	5.7	8743	255.6

27004 JUNO waits at the head of a service from Manchester which has just arrived at Victoria's platform 4 on a damp, and cold Saturday 8th December 1962. This may well have been a Liverpool-Hull train, or even the Harwich boat train, either of which the Co-Co would have powered from Guide Bridge. Once uncoupled the EM2 would make its way to a short siding near to the Victoria hotel at the west end of the station to await the next Down working. The constant shuttling between Manchester and Sheffield enabled these locomotives to chalk up some respectable mileage's each year although JUNO had the lowest accumulative total from new up to October 1960 when 414,047 miles were recorded; others had passed the half million mark by then! In 1961 it managed 76,811 miles, whilst in 1960 it scored the lowest ever for the class with just 48,801 miles. However, it was the last of the class to be scrapped by the Dutch railways, finally succumbing in October 1986. None of the class exceeded 800,000 miles during BR service. ***A.Ives (ARPT).***

With 76021 for company, 76013 took part in the *ACDC* railtour on 16th September 1978. The pair were seen at Piccadilly station Manchester with a group of fashion conscious admirers. Sadly, mileage records from this period do not seem to exist. ***Norman Preedy.***

AVERAGE ANNUAL MILEAGE PER LOCOMOTIVE

Analysis of Weekdays:

Key: (1) Class. (2) Number of locomotives in class. (3) Average annual miles. (4) Days in main works. (5) Examination and running repairs [days]. (6) Total. (7) Available but not required. (8) Total 'out of service' days. (9) Days in service. (10) Percentage of 100%. 'A' - LM 3,300 hp Bo-Bo electric locomotive, a type covering several classes.

1951

No figures available for EM1 class but 309 days was calculated to be the average period for not being required. At 31/12/51 twenty-six locomotives were available for traffic.

1952 (Eastern Region)

(1)	(2)	(3)	(4)	(5)	(6)	(7)	(8)	(9)	(10)
EM1	52	14544	39	20	59	121	180	129	41.7%

Note: *26 locos added.*

For a minor comparison, the two ex-North Eastern Railway Bo-Bo electric locomotives 26500 and 26501 averaged 15,378 miles, they were in service for 161 weekdays and out of service for 148 weekdays, which equats to 52.1% availabiity.

1953 (Eastern Region)

(1)	(2)	(3)	(4)	(5)	(6)	(7)	(8)	(9)	(10)
EM1	58	13405	15	2	17	151	168	147	46.6%
EM2	1	—	—	—	—	—	—	—	—

1954 (Eastern Region)

(1)	(2)	(3)	(4)	(5)	(6)	(7)	(8)	(9)	(10)
EM1	58	25826	17	1	18	72	90	219	71%
EM2	7	29306	—	—	—	81	81	228	74%

1955 (Eastern Region)

(1)	(2)	(3)	(4)	(5)	(6)	(7)	(8)	(9)	(10)
EM1	58	42846	15	—	15	15	30	279	90%
EM2	7	66865	34	1	35	14	49	260	84%

1956 (Eastern Region)

(1)	(2)	(3)	(4)	(5)	(6)	(7)	(8)	(9)	(10)
EM1	58	43020	23	4	27	2	29	280	91%
EM2	7	75697	35	2	37	1	38	271	88%

1957

(1)	(2)	(3)	(4)	(5)	(6)	(7)	(8)	(9)	(10)

No figures available for this period.

1958 (London Midland Region)

(1)	(2)	(3)	(4)	(5)	(6)	(7)	(8)	(9)	(10)
EM1	58	42996	16	1	17	2	19	290	94%
EM2	7	66406	62	2	64	3	67	242	78%

1959 (London Midland Region)

(1)	(2)	(3)	(4)	(5)	(6)	(7)	(8)	(9)	(10)
EM1	58	42361	25	1	26	2	28	287	91%
EM2	7	75141	23	10	33	3	36	279	89%
'A'	*New during year.*								

1960 (London Midland Region)

(1)	(2)	(3)	(4)	(5)	(6)	(7)	(8)	(9)	(10)
EM1	58	40820	21	5	26	3	29	280	91%
EM2	7	66946	32	6	38	1	39	270	87%
'A'	41	11101	157	5	162	21	183	126	41%

1961 (London Midland Region)

(1)	(2)	(3)	(4)	(5)	(6)	(7)	(8)	(9)	(10)
EM1	58	39493	19	14	33	2	35	274	89%
EM2	7	71489	27	9	36	2	38	271	88%
'A'	64	12476	50	82	132	73	205	104	34%

DAYS OUT OF SERVICE 1958-61: Including days awaiting works; days on works; running repairs and exams; days not required, and days stored (figures in italics are days at main works only, other figures are unknown). Weekdays only are included in the calculations.

LOCO	1958	1959	1960	1961
26000	175	47	9	—
26001	0	20	3	—
26002	63	67	36	—
26003	2	15	56	—
26004	13	0	56	—
26005	28	5	6	*61*
26006	1	22	1	*73*
26007	19	1	12	*60*
26008	46	4	11	*40*
26009	0	17	49	—
26010	1	39	44	—
26011	3	11	3	*45*
26012	1	15	58	—
26013	1	78	17	—
26014	9	69	10	—
26015	123	5	11	—
26016	35	35	26	—
26017	3	6	12	—
26018	32	32	40	—
26019	40	0	22	—
26020	7	84	7	—
26021	6	92	8	—
26022	31	79	4	—
26023	0	5	60	—
26024	1	17	63	—
26025	12	18	6	—
26026	73	8	51	—
26027	4	13	58	—
26028	18	*47*	*2*	—
26029	0	*45*	*1*	—
26030	7	0	*64*	*16*
26031	0	*5*	*14*	*32*
26032	35	*44*	*7*	*2*

LOCO	1958	1959	1960	1961
26033	35	*45*	*0*	*6*
26034	0	*85*	*0*	*6*
26035	0	0	*51*	—
26036	22	0	*44*	*1*
26037	0	*70*	*2*	*12*
26038	5	*14*	*33*	*16*
26039	20	*3*	*34*	—
26040	0	*1*	*35*	—
26041	0	*14*	*36*	*6*
26042	17	*0*	*5*	*72*
26043	6	*0*	*38*	—
26044	1	*58*	*1*	—
26045	8	*0*	*55*	—
26046	0	*80*	*8*	—
26047	0	*11*	*52*	*9*
26048	27	*0*	*67*	*3*
26049	26	*24*	*58*	*29*
26050	19	*0*	*56*	—
26051	11	*14*	*2*	*44*
26052	43	*50*	*1*	*59*
26053	34	0	*50*	*15*
26054	11	*32*	*1*	—
26055	2	*30*	*4*	*64*
26056	0	*44*	*1*	*60*
26057	60	*0*	*64*	—
27000	53	*27*	*0*	*35*
27001	67	*25*	*41*	—
27002	59	*18*	*21*	*61*
27003	62	*8*	*31*	*16*
27004	53	*23*	*91*	—
27005	119	*20*	*59*	—
27006	55	*48*	*3*	*10*

27004 pulls away from the platforms at Manchester London Road after being released from a Down working on Sunday 10th July 1955. Sunday working must have boosted the mileage figures for this class but the constant to-and-fro over Woodhead was the key. ***K.R.Pirt.***

With the wires raised for the road crossing clearance at Torside, 27005 stretches its pantographs skywards as it whisks the Liverpool (Central)–Harwich (Parkeston Quay) boat train up 'the bank' towards Woodhead on the afternoon of Saturday 17th March 1956. This was a regular working for the EM2s as the train was loaded with at least eight bogies daily and year round too. The Co-Cos met the train at Guide Bridge after it had run through the southern suburbs of Manchester steam hauled from Manchester (Central). Interestingly, that train was never diesel hauled over that short section from Central. *Norman Preedy.*

26017 and 26023 work through Barnsley junction, Penistone on an unknown date in the Fifties'! *Transport Treasury.*

Off to another job and clocking up more mileage, 76009 and a sister run through Guide Bridge on 30th March 1977 after servicing at Reddish. ***Norman Preedy.***

Dual-braked 76029 waits for a service at Reddish on 2nd July 1978. Coal dust from the intensive MGR workings tended to gather slowly on these locomotives until it became unsightly. ***Hugh P.Searle.***

THE MAKING OF AN EM2 Co-Co

(opposite, bottom) **Believed to be 27000 in the making! With the various compartments already created and equipment being installed. In the adjacent bay at Gorton, ex-LNER steam locomotives of Class O4 undergo overhaul. *E.M.Johnson coll.***

(opposite, top) **The main frames for an EM2 are laid out in the erecting shop at Gorton. No jigs required it seems! Measure, measure again, cut, secure with clamps, and then weld the I-beams. Unlike the EM1s, the main frame of the Co-Co played an integral part in the transmission of forces with the drawgear attached to the frame whilst the bogies were independent of each other but attached to the main frame. *E.M.Johnson coll.***

(left) **It will be some time before a locomotive will emerge but we get the idea from this aspect with the buffer beams fitted. *E.M.Johnson coll.***

(below and bottom) **Gorton 1953: One of the six-wheel bogies is virtually ready to receive the three traction motors but that event would be some time in the future. Lots of other bits and pieces have yet to be fitted including the distinctive air tanks. Note that the inside surfaces of the bogie frame has been painted black prior to installation of the motors. In BR service these bogies developed hair-line fractures because of insufficient side-play on the middle axle. *E.M.Johnson coll.***

The south bay of the erecting shop at Gorton works on Monday 16th March 1953. EM2 No.27000, with its temporary numbering style and in a primer coat of paint, is progressing towards completion but it would be late December before the big Co-Co was released to traffic. However, there was no requirement to rush these locomotives into work because the MSW system was itself far from ready to accept the express passenger services that they would serve. Still in bare metal, sister No.27001 is on the left and would be some three months behind the class doyen before it too was put to work. *Transport Treasury.*

Somewhere near Penistone, 27000 effortlessly works (admitted, it is going downhill) an UP express of mainly Mk.1 carriages. The Co-Co is still in black livery and beginning to show some weathering so the image could have been recorded at any time between mid-1954 and mid-1956. *Authors coll.*

CLASS EM2 (TOPS CLASS 77) - The Works Record

27000

Built Gorton.
To traffic: 28/12/53.
Works No.1065.

Renumbered: E27000 – 24/7/66.

Repairs:
Gorton 23/3–9/4/55 **CH** (46,023 miles);
Gorton 6/7-25/8/56 **CL** (147,268 miles);
Gorton 15-26/1/57 **CL** (173,165 miles);
Gorton 23/2-16/3/57 **CL** (182,085 miles);
Gorton 2/12/57-12/3/58 **CH** (246,909 miles);
Gorton 27/11-5/12/58 **CL** (308,099 miles);
Gorton 27/7-17/8/59 **CH** [cost £3,299] (364,471 miles);
Gorton 30/11-10/12/59 **CL** [cost £493] (387,111 miles);
Gorton 28/4-8/6/61 **CH** (501,317 miles);
Gorton <15/12/62>;
Gorton <3/3/63>;
Crewe 26/1-11/2/64>;
Crewe 29/5-24/7/66;
Taken out of traffic: 2/3/68.
Stored: Bury 16/3-5/10/68.
Withdrawn: 5/10/68.

27000 inside the servicing shed at Reddish depot on Sunday 23rd September 1956. By now the EM2 has acquired lined green livery and wears the large BR lion-and-wheel emblem. It will be noted that this section of the depot was wired throughout enabling testing of any locomotive's on-board equipment to be carried out with minimum fuss. All the servicing procedures required staff to work either inside the locomotive or outside below body level only, except for cab windows and screen wipers. *D.Fairley*.

This image shows 27000 attending an exhibition at, apparently, Rochdale on Saturday 6th October 1956. Reddish, or was it Gorton, have given the locomotive a superb clean, polish and touch-up with the paint brush, to exhibition standard. This writer has found no record of this exhibition but the stock – a BR Standard locomotive tender (new ex-Horwich?) is just visible on the left and what appears to be an Engineers saloon is buffered up on the right – must have been accommodated in one of the bays at the east end of the station. The flags suggest that the event had some connection with the Commonwealth but the annual commemoration of that organisation usually falls in March! Answers please, via the usual channels. *Transport Treasury*.

(below) **An undated view of 27000 at Sheffield (Victoria) shortly after the Co-Co had backed onto a Down working on platform 3. Nicely captured by this illustration is a brief moment of pure history. The secondman/fireman is observing the work of the shunter coupling the engine to the train, whilst beyond them, the activity centres around porters loading parcels whilst passengers appear to be coming and going. It seems that the train is a through working from Hull, Cleethorpes, or elsewhere; the time shown on the clock is 4.25 p.m. so it can't be the Harwich-Liverpool service – unless it was very late running. 27000 was still in the all-black as built livery, with copious amounts of road dirt embellishing the lower body. Note legend EM2 is just visible amongst the filth on the bufferbeam. *Transport Treasury*.**

In July 1959, just weeks before it was named ELECTRA, 27000 is stabled in the stub siding alongside the Victoria Hotel, and is ready and waiting to relieve 'Director' 62661 on a westbound working from Sheffield which originated in Cleethorpes. ***A.R.Thompson (ARPT).***

27000 ELECTRA running light at Manchester (Piccadilly), Thursday 25th June 1964. The green livery is taking on a beige tone from the road dirt clinging all along the lower body. None of the class got anything larger than the yellow warning panel as here. ***David Christie.***

27001

Built Gorton.
To traffic: 22/3/54.
Works No.1066.

Repairs:
Gorton 3-6/1/55 **NC**;
Gorton 17-20/1/55 **NC**;
Gorton 5/4-14/5/55 **CH** (49,645 miles);
Gorton 5-19/11/55 **CL** (85,057 miles);
Gorton 15/8-29/9/56 **CH** (149,702 miles);
Gorton 10/4-14/6/58 **CH** [cost £2,708] (284,405 miles);
Gorton 7-9/7/58 **NC**;
Gorton 19-29/1/59 **CL** [cost £154] (335,460 miles);
Gorton 23-26/3/59 **CL** [cost £54] (346,856 miles);
Gorton 14-29/9/59 **CL** [cost £311] (383,375 miles);
Gorton 5-28/1/60 **CH** [cost £2,785] (404,673 miles);
Gorton 8-13/9/60 **CL** [cost £366] (448,067 miles);
Gorton 12/11-2/12/60 **CL** [cost £386] (460,221 miles);
Gorton 17-28/4/61 **CL**;
Gorton 1/5-4/8/61 *Weigh*;
Gorton 26/10-19/12/61 **CH**;
Gorton <15/12/62>;
Gorton <27/5/63 **CL** *Last locomotive repaired at Gorton;*
Crewe <10/11/63>;
Crewe <30/1/66>;
Taken out of traffic: 2/3/68.
Stored: Bury 16/3-5/10/68.
Withdrawn: 5/10/68.

Early days: 27001 runs into Sheffield (Victoria) with an express from Manchester as a 'matt black' EM1 heads west, light engine. *C.J.B.Sanderson (ARPT).*

Although not of the best quality, this illustration deserves a place within this tome by dint of the fact that the EM2s were something of a rarity around Wath - eventually. This view shows Nos.27002 and 27001 at the south end of the siding where EM1s were normally stabled for their weekends in what was essentially one of the most polluted environments in Yorkshire (which had nothing to do with the quality of the picture but the ever present murk is noticeable). The date is 20th June 1954, a Sunday, and some nine days after its return from London, 27002 still carries the exhibition finish from its three-week attendance at the Willesden 'do'. The big engines were tried out on the Wath branch working both empty and loaded trains but their braking deficiencies were soon discovered. One former driver described working a freight train with 27002, during the formative years of the MSW, as 'quite hair-raising' and never repeated the experience. At times of coal shortages (and there were many during the early decades of nationalisation) Wath yard and the electrified route to the west became rather busy with coal traffic and to get the trains up to Penistone, allsorts of motive power would be employed to bank the EM1s located on the front of the trains; EM2s would sometimes be called to lend a hand. *Transport Treasury.*

On what some might describe as a typical Manchester day, 27001 waits at the head of an eastbound service on the last day of July 1954. The black finish afforded the MSW locomotives soon gave way to the rigours of the weather and the 'residue' generated by the overhead contact of pantograph and wires but it would be a couple of years before lined green livery was introduced to give a longer lasting 'clean' look. *Norman Preedy.*

An undated view of 27001 receiving attention on the track which was dedicated for electric locomotive testing and was located alongside the south wall of the erecting shop at Gorton. By now the Co-Co has lined green livery but is yet to be named, so it is pre-September 1959. Note that the train heating hose has been disconnected from the bufferbeam; which was a standard summertime occurrence in these parts. As for the removal of the body panel, it appears that work concerning the boiler is taking place. I wonder what was in the pristine cardboard box discarded on the ground? *Norman Preedy*. *(below)* **27001 ARIADNE, in blue livery with a yellow warning panel, has charge of a Sheffield working at Manchester (Piccadilly) in June 1966. From early 1957 lined Brunswick (some observers describe as Olive) green livery was introduced for this class, the lining consisting orange and black. Between May and October 1959, nameplates were fitted to all but 27003 which had to wait until January 1961 before it was named. *Authors coll.***

27002

Built Gorton.
To traffic: 18/5/54.
Works No.1067.
On loan to Willesden Exhibition 18/5/54 to 10/6/54.

Repairs:
Gorton 3-23/4/55 **CL** (45,849 miles);
Gorton 15/10-12/11/55 **CH** (78,420 miles);
Gorton 29/12/55-25/2/56 **CL** (89,457 miles);
Gorton 11/5-8/6/57 **CH** (190,419 miles);
Gorton 8-10/7/57 **NC**;
Gorton 12/3-9/4/58 **CL** [cost £1,028] (249,377 miles);
Gorton 10/7/58 **NC**;
Gorton 18/11/58-19/2/59 **CH** [cost £2,663] (302,565 mles);
Gorton 16-25/6/59 **NC** (327,818 miles);
Gorton 30/9-12/10/59 **CL** [cost £569] (348,310 miles);
Gorton 1-22/2/60 **NC** (371,723 miles);
Gorton 28/4-2/5/60 **NC** (383,662 miles);
Gorton 16-19/1/61 **NC** (437,445 miles);
Gorton 26-27/1/61 **NC** (437,624 miles);
Gorton 24/3-10/4/61 **CL** [cost £361] (440,634 miles);
Gorton 16/8-4/10/61 **CH** (478,767 miles);
Gorton 8-10/11/61 **NC** (486,070 miles);
Gorton <27/5/62>;
Crewe 22/6-18/12/63;
Crewe <7-14/11/65>;
Crewe <21/5/67>;
Taken out of traffic: 2/3/68.
Stored: Bury 16/3-5/10/68.
Withdrawn: 5/10/68.

The rivets are highlighted by the morning sun as 27002 leaves the dock line at Sheffield's Victoria station on 16th August 1955 prior to coupling onto a westbound working. There would have been no requirement to top-up the heating boiler tank on this warm summer day. *Transport Treasury.*

With disc type express headcode at the ready, but for reasons unknown, 27002 was stabled, awaiting a westbound working, at Penistone of all places in 1955. Note that the Co-Co is unusually dirty. ***C.J.B.Sanderson (ARPT).***

On an unrecorded date, 27002 stands on the middle road between platforms 3 and 4 at Sheffield (Victoria). This locomotive was to lead something of a charmed life similar in some respects to that led by EM1 No.26020. Celebrity status was accorded initially when it went to the Willesden exhibition. Later it was the motive power for some high profile rail tours but after it left the UK in 1969 its status waned and in 1985 after fifteen years working for the Dutch railways (longer than the time on BR note), it was scrapped. ***C.J.B.Sanderson (ARPT).***

Days of shiny black livery and no nameplates: 27002 slows for the stop at Dunford Bridge station with an *Ian Allan Pullman* special on 12th May 1956. *J.W.Armstrong (ARPT).* *(below)* **In a scene which would be totally alien on today's railways, enthusiasts who have alighted from what appears to be the *Ian Allan Pullman Railtour*, stand around the front end of EM2 27002 as an Up freight passes by with an unidentified EM1 at its head. The location is Dunford Bridge, looking west towards the eastern portal of the Woodhead tunnel on 12th May 1956. Imagine the surprise/horror on the Bo+Bo crews' faces as they exited the tunnel, or were they pre-warned of the throng? *J.W.Armstrong (ARPT).***

During their sojourn at Sheffield waiting for westbound (Down) passenger workings, the EM2s, and EM1s, sat out the time in the dock line on the south side of Victoria station. 27002 and her crew wait during a September afternoon in 1957. *Transport Treasury*. *(below)* **Sporting its lined green livery and the new BR crest, 27002 is released from its Up train at Sheffield on Saturday 26th April 1958. Besides the Manchester–Sheffield 'shuttles' the Woodhead route also saw frequent passenger services running between Liverpool (Central) and Hull (Paragon), the daily return boat train between Liverpool (Central) and Harwich (Parkeston Quay), Manchester (London Road/Piccadilly) services to Cleethorpes, and London services to Marylebone. Even with its speed restrictions, the Woodhead route was the fastest means between Sheffield and Manchester, far superior to the Hope valley line! *W.R.E.Lewis (ARPT)*.**

Waiting to be released from platform 4 at Manchester (Piccadilly) on Wednesday 14th June 1961, 27002 AURORA wears the fully lined green livery which was to give way to the electric blue. However, that was a couple of years hence once Crewe had taken over maintenance of the class. *Transport Treasury*. *(below)* **The great bulk of the EM2 design is depicted nicely here by 27002 outside the repair shop at Reddish on 3rd July 1966. The all over blue livery appeared, for some reason, to suit the class more than the diesel locomotives which were later to acquire the corporate blue. Common to both the EM1 and EM2 classes, when stabled with the pantographs in contact with overhead, the compressors were continually cutting in and 'ticking away' to keep the air tanks topped-up. *A.Ives (ARPT).***

27003

Built Gorton.
To traffic: 5/8/54.
Works No.1068.

Renumbered: E27003 - 22/1/67.

Repairs:
Gorton 7/5-25/10/55 **CH** (46,103 miles);
Gorton 30/11-24/12/55 **CH** (83,275 miles);
Gorton 5/9-11/10/56 **CL** (140,432 miles);
Gorton 2/1-9/2/57 **CH** (158,316 miles);
Gorton 29/5-8/6/57 **CH** (180,717 miles);
Gorton 3/9-13/11/58 **CH** [cost £2,844] (289,842 miles);
Gorton 15-24/4/59 **CL** [cost £188] (325,966 miles);
Gorton 20-25/2/60 **CL** [cost £2,759] (395,398 miles);
Gorton 19-22/10/60 **NC** (443,311 miles);
Gorton 1/12/60-10/1/61 **CH** [cost £3,194] (452,049 miles);
Gorton 22-25/7/61 **CL** (495,862 miles);
Gorton 18-25/10/61 **CL** (513,053 miles);
Gorton 1/9-14/10/62 **HG**;
Crewe <25/3-18/4/64>;
Crewe <18/12/66-22/1/67>;
Taken out of traffic: 2/3/68.
Stored: Bury 16/3-5/10/68.
Withdrawn: 5/10/68.

Standing in platform 3 at Sheffield (Victoria) station, 27003 is ready to depart with a Down working for Manchester on Saturday morning 14th September 1957. This EM2 was the last of the class to be named, an event which took place some eighteen months or so after the rest of the Co-Cos had acquired their names. DIANA was the name chosen for 27003. *C.J.B.Sanderson (ARPT).*

27004

Built Gorton.
To traffic: 18/9/54.
Works No.1069.

Renumbered: E27004 - 1/10/67.

Repairs:
Gorton 20/3-7/4/55 **CL** (31,852 miles);
Gorton 23/6-2/7/55 **CL** (44,709 miles);
Gorton 14/4-27/5/56 **CH** (109,611 miles);
Gorton 19/10-9/11/57 **CL** (217,530 miles);
Gorton 27/10/58-15/1/59 **CH** (298,540 miles);
Gorton 12-17/6/59 **NC** (332,457 miles);
Gorton 17-24/11/59 **CH** [cost £3,717] (366,048 miles);
Gorton 22/2-13/4/60 **CH** [cost £420](382,220 miles);
Gorton 3/10-26/11/60 **CL** [cost £374] (414,047 miles);
Gorton <14/10/62>;
Gorton <3/3/63>;
Crewe <15/11/63> HG,
Crewe <20/9/64>;
Crewe <21/3/65>;
Crewe 27/8-1/10/67>;
Taken out of traffic: 2/3/68.
Stored: Bury 16/3-5/10/68
Withdrawn: 5/10/68.

Standing at platform 2 with a westbound service, 27004 has its 320-gallon heating water tank topped up at Victoria station on that cold, wet Saturday in December 1962. Such an operation was a two man job, with the stop valve and hose tidily accommodated inside the manhole on the platform. The Driver/Motorman can be seen connecting the hose to the intake valve on the locomotive – note the cloud of steam above – whilst the Secondman, controlling the on-off valve, is just visible with his head and shoulders above the manhole cover. Note the absence of any guard rails or signs warning passengers to watch their step. It was expected that common sense and observation would come into play in those pre-H&SE days. *A.Ives (ARPT).*

On a somewhat earlier but unrecorded date, 27004 is backing onto its next Down working at the west end of Sheffield (Victoria) station. The sandboxes look like a force to be reckoned with! ***N.E.Stead coll.***

Now in all over blue livery, EM2 No.27004 JUNO stands outside the north end of the servicing shed Reddish depot circa 1965 before the yellow warning panels were applied to the front faces. ***Authors coll.***

27005

Built Gorton.
To traffic: 11/12/54.
Works No.1070.

Renumbered: E27005 - 11/9/66.

Repairs:
Gorton 20/6-9/7/55 **CH** (35,532 miles);
Gorton 9/11-29/12/56 **CH** (146,797 miles);
Gorton 2/6-30/8/58 **CH** [cost £3,229] (267,218 miles);
Gorton 21/10-7/11/58 **CL** [cost £824] (279,691 miles);
Gorton 21/1-3/2/59 **CL** [cost £79] (298,747 miles);
Gorton 19-29/5/59 **NC** (323,829 miles);
Gorton 13/6-11/8/60 **CH** [cost £3,819] (405,701 miles);
Gorton 25/10-3/11/60 **CL** [cost £151] (421,758 miles);
Gorton <26/5/63>;
Crewe 30/8-12/10/64;
Crewe 24/7-9/10/66;
Taken out of traffic: 2/3/68.
Stored: Bury 16/3-5/10/68.
Withdrawn: 5/10/68.

Uncoupled and about to pull away from its stock, recently named 27005 MINERVA has just arrived in Sheffield with yet another express from Manchester. The date is sometime during July 1959 with a slight drizzle adding to the gloom of Victoria's atmosphere. This was the only member of the class not to work on the railway system in the Netherlands and instead ended up providing spares for the rest of the class. *A.R.Thompson (ARPT).*

On another somewhat sunnier, and later, occasion, MINERVA is at the head of another passenger working at Sheffield. It will be noticed that the Metro-Vic worksplate is far from central to the bodyline. *Transport Treasury.*

Still in green livery, E27005 MINERVA is buffered up to a strange bedfellow at Reddish on 14th May 1967 in the shape of ex-LMS jackshaft diesel-electric 350 h.p. 0-6-0 shunter No.12024 from Newton Heath depot. Many different diesel locomotive types came to Reddish over the operational lifetime of the depot, mainly for wheel turning on the 'state-of-the-art' lathe. *A.Ives (ARPT).*

27006

Built Gorton.
To traffic: 31/12/54.
Works No.1071.

Renumbered: E27006 - 18/12/66.

Repairs:
Gorton 2/7-13/8/55 **CL** (34,862 miles);
Gorton 11/6-7/7/56 **CH** (102,465 miles);
Gorton 26/9-12/10/57 **CH** (200,847 miles);
Gorton 16/5-11/7/58 **CH** [cost £1,711] (252,128 miles);
Gorton 28/7-1/8/58 **NC** (252,659 miles);
Gorton 12/1-6/2/59 **NC** (291,834 miles);
Gorton 1-15/4/59 **CH** [cost £2,487] (303,671 miles);
Gorton 30/4-2/5/59 **NC** (306,997 miles);
Gorton 4-9/6/59 **NC** (313,416 miles);
Gorton 26/6-7/7/59 **CL** (317,535 miles);
Gorton 24-26/10/60 **CL** [cost £59] (420,427 miles);
Gorton 14-26/9/61 **CL** (488,081 miles);
Crewe <1/5-14/8/64>;
Crewe <20/11-18/12/66>;
Taken out of traffic: 2/3/68.
Stored: Bury 16/3-5/10/68.
Withdrawn: 5/10/68.

Numerous photographers have captured departing GC line expresses waiting for the 'off' at this location on the east side of the old London Road station before the rebuilding of the late Fifties'/early Sixties'. This is yet to be named EM2 27006 with a London (Marylebone) service on Saturday 18th June 1955. The agility of the Secondman is tested whilst he cleans the windscreen; would such practice be allowed today? In the siding beyond is EM1 26053 waiting to 'back on' the next Sheffield service. *F.W.Hampson (ARPT).*

Just west of Penistone, 27006 enters a cutting as it coasts downhill with an express in 1957. Up to this time, the livery was black with red, cream and grey lining. *Book Law coll.*

Complete with lined green livery and fairly new PANDORA nameplates, 27006 stands in the works yard at Gorton on Sunday 28th June 1959. Having arrived on the previous Friday, the EM2 was in works for a Casual Light repair (26th June to 7th July). Celebrity 26020 had just arrived in shops for a Heavy General overhaul at which lined green livery was applied. *Unknown photographer.*

(above) **27006 stands at platform 1 in Piccadilly station on the evening of Saturday 18th June 1966 after arrival with a service from Sheffield.** ***Norman Preedy.***

GOING DUTCH!

(right) **Continuing in passenger service in Holland, EM2 27006 in its new guise as NS 1504. The NS were appropriately searching for suitable electric locomotives in 1969 when the seven EM2s were available at a knock-down price. On Wednesday 20th August 1969 E27002 ran with a five-coach special train (1X36) from Reddish depot to Sheffield Victoria and back with NS representatives on board. The sale was made and the entire class shipped over to Holland just weeks later when on 25th September the class was loaded aboard the motor vessel *Cambridge Ferry* at Harwich, sailing to Zeebrugge. E27002 was initially used as the 'test piece' whilst the others waited their turn to enter Tilburg locomotive works for conversion to NS standards. E27003 was the first in November 1969, emerging six months later in its new livery as NS 1501. E27005 was found to be in such a condition as to be not worth rebuilding and was scrapped to provide spares for the other six. E27002, after its period of varying trials, was the final one to be rebuilt and entered traffic on 24th June 1971 as NS 1506.** ***Authors coll.***

REPATRIATION!

(above) **27001 as NS 1505. Returned to the United Kingdom after withdrawal in Holland, this locomotive is now a major attraction at Manchester's Museum of Science & Industry, albeit in Dutch livery. However, 27000 (NS 1502) was another of the class which made it back home and is in the care of the EM2 Society, restored to its BR green lined livery .** ***Photographer unknown.*** *(below)* **NS1502 on display at Highley SVR on 11th October 1987 after repatriation to England.** ***Norman Preedy.***

NS1502 had been on display at the Basingstoke exhibition a few weeks earlier. The BR Timken axlebox covers have been painted for our delectation and the nameplate is in place. Note also that the Metro-Vic plate is not only still in situ but is undisturbed. ***Norman Preedy.***

27001 ARIADNE, in its guise as NS 1505, stands outside the Manchester Museum of Science & Industry at Liverpool Road station on 1st March 1992, after its return from Holland. The nameplates have been re-affixed for the homecoming and certain of the fitting necessary for working on the NS system – such as the massive sand boxes – have been removed. ***Hugh P.Searle.***

SOME DETAIL

This section is aimed not just at the historian; it is probably just as important to the modellers who want their model to reflect the prototype at the period represented. Obviously these lists are not exhaustive and are gleaned not only from the scant official sources but in the main from photographic observation covering most of the locomotives of each class at varying periods of their operational lives. Of course, it would require an illustration of every locomotive at every stage of its life (virtually every year) to collate a more accurate picture of what was carried out. It would be safe to say that not all changes affected every locomotive and existing BR records do not reveal what might be regarded as minor detail changes (those that did were long ago destroyed). Therefore, this writer can only repeat the advice often given to modellers: If total accuracy is required, acquire as many images of the subject as it is possible to collect, hunt down articles in magazines, look at specific books. This might be regarded as 'rivet counting' nowadays but it is sound advice and will be worth the trouble to get things right.

MULTIPLE UNIT WORKING

One major 'detail' change was the fitting of equipment to a large number of the EM1 class to enable Multiple Unit operations to be carried out. Outwardly this changed the front-end appearance of the locomotives concerned when jumper cables adorned the cabs. All of those had air brakes fitted and many became dual-braked. However, some of the later conversions had their vacuum brake equipment taken out and they then lost the vacuum hoses at each end – another difference! It was usual that MU-fitted locomotives worked in pairs for lengthy periods and it was rare to see them working alone whereas the vacuum only engines worked independently. The locomotives involved and the dates they were converted is given in the individual locomotive tables so there is little need to list that information here.

TRAIN HEATING BOILERS:

On the EM1 class the boilers were fitted at the No.2 end of the locomotive in the compartment immediately below the left inside corner of the pantograph. A removable panel (fitted with a window and small size ventilator) depicted the compartment in the bodyside. Just below the panel was a hole to allow a hose pipe to fill the 240 gallon water tank. A drain pipe, with a bulbous end, hung below the body just after the boiler compartment (mid bogie for clearance) in front of the jacking brackets.

Boilers were fitted to the following from new:-

26000	
26050	removed 6/77.
26051	removed 12/70.
26052	left in situ.
26053	removed 10/70.
26054	left in situ.
26055	left in situ.
26056	removed 11/70.
26057	removed 7/72.

Boilers fitted later:

26020	2/55	removed 2/66 (refitted at Reddish, July 77 prior to preservation)
26046	9/55	removed 10/63
26047	5/55	removed 10/63
26048	4/55	removed 11/63
26049	7/55	removed c9/70 (boiler taken out during period 11/55 to 3/56 and re-installed)

EM2 class, which were all fitted from new and kept them to the end of BR operations, also had their train heating boilers at No.2 end, in a compartment below the pantograph.

76029, one of the early conversions to MU-working, displays the vacuum hose which remained in place. *Hugh P.Searle.*

76033, a later conversion (May 1976), presents a cleaner face to the camera. *Hugh P.Searle.*

CAB ROOF RAIN STRIPS:

One of the more obscure changes which created variations in appearance over the life of the classes was the humble rain strip(s) on the cab roof. There were various strips in use on the cab section of the roofs over the years and the initial batch of EM1s appear to have had no rain strips fitted at first (although 26000 had small strips over the doorways when built, when sent to Holland, and were the only examples 26000 had throughout its life). This attention to minor detail might be regarded by some as superfluous (most of the minor detail regarding the EM1s was just that) but nevertheless it is worth listing because, from an elevated aspect especially, the EM1s had quiet distinctive and different rain strips over the years. Even from platform level they could be spotted, although not so easily from ground level. However, most models are viewed from above so the roof detail is somewhat important after all! Illustrations of all the listed examples of strips can be found throughout this volume but images in this section will hopefully give inspiration to get things right from the outset.

At the end, 1981, both 76028 and 76029 had curved strips at both ends, on both sides, over the cab door/side window section only, as did the following at the dates shown:
26001 and 76001 at 30/5/54 and 13/11/79.
26002 at 12/11/50 and 15/4/55.
26003, E26003 and 76003 at 18/7/52, 11/69, 5/74, 13/11/79.
76006 at 22/4/76.
76007 at 4/7/78 and 24/7/80.
26008 and 76008 at 1/9/77.
76009 at 25/2/81.
76010 at 10/78 (*see* also below).
76011 at 1/9/73.
76012 at 24/7/80.
26013 and 76013 at 7/6/53 and 30/12/80 (*see* also below).
26015 at 9/7/54.
76015 at 26/4/81.
26016 and 76016 at 30/5/54 and 14/10/78.
26017 at 4/2/52.
26019 at 1951.
26020 and 76020 at 3/6/54 and 10/9/77.
26021 and 76021 at c 1953 and 16/9/78.
26022 at 19/6/52.
26023 and 76023 at 19/9/54 and 10/78.
76024 at 11/12/79 (*see* also below).
26025 and 76025 at 19/6/52, 28/3/75 and 26/3/81.
26026 and 76026 circa 1954 (*see* below also) and 11/12/79.
26027 at 27/8/55.
26028 and 76028 at 21/5/53 and 3/81.
26029 and 76029 at 19/9/54 and 16/5/77 (*see* also below).
76030 at 7/74.
26031 at 16/3/65.
26032 at 14/8/52.
26034 and 76034 at 1952, 19/9/54 and 10/8/79.
76035 at 26/2/81.
26036 (*see* also below).
76037 at 25/3/81.
26040 at 14/3/53 (*see* also below).
26041 at 7/10/54.
26046 (*see* also below).
76047 at 4/80.
76051 at 14/8/75 and 23/9/80.
76052 at 21/4/76 (*see* also below).
26053 and 76053 at 18/8/67 and 3/81.

(top) **26000 displays the rather subtle rain stips located above each doorway. These remained in situ throughout TOMMY's life.** *(above)* **26005 had no rain strips in 1955. *K.R.Pirt.***

26054 at 4/6/54.
26055 at 4/5/68 (*see also* below).
26056 at 20/6/54.

18th April 1964 – 26050 had distinctive and easily recognisable, eyebrow type rain strips above each front window, running diagonally front to side, with a connecting strip leading off to the rear of the cab behind the door. As did the following at the recorded dates:
E26033 and 76033 at 8/9/69, 20/9/78 and 11/1/80.
26037 at 21/5/53.
76038 (ex 26050) at 26/2/81.
76040 at 26/2/81 (*see* also below).
26049 and 76049 at 8/68 and 8/8/78.
E26050 at 14/3/70.

26021 and 26029 in July 1955 display the same rain strip pattern which they appeaar to have got from new. ***K.R.Pirt.***

Two views of EM2s in 1955 displaying the three-piece rain strips they were equipped with from the start. ***K.R.Pirt.***

West of Penistone in 1956, No.26043 has the three-piece pattern rain strip. ***Book Law coll.***

E26026 had a continuous rain strip at the front of each cab (rising towards the centre horns, like a receding hairline) with connecting side strips over each doorway. As did the following on the dates recorded:
26005 at 21/7/55 (ex works) and 1964.
26007 mid 1960s.
26009 at c 1955.
76010 at 3/80.
26012 but no date.
26013 and 76013 at c1956 and 25/2/81.
26018 at 3/4/69.
26020 at 26/2/55.
26021 at 17/7/55.
26022 and 76022 at c1955 and 3/81.
26024 at c1955.
26029 at 17/7/55 and 31/5/59 (*see* also above).
26032 at 1953
26033 at c1954 and 16/8/55.
26036 at 27/8/55 and c 1960 (*see* also above).
26039 at circa 1955.
26040 and 76040 at 3/57, 8/9/69 and 2/6/78 (*see* above).
26043 but no date.
76046 at 21/4/79.
26052 at c1956.
26055 at 2/5/55.

Another type of rain strip was worn by E26046 at 5th April 1969. This type was parallel to the front windows some six inches above and spanning the width of the cab. Connecting arch side strips (as per standard) protected the doorways. Eight years earlier, on 29th October 1961, No.26046 had yet a different type of rain strip over both cabs. This was similar to the receding hairline (or reverse basin cut) type but did not connect with the doorway strips at either end by approximately 12 inches.

26049 had not only a continuous strip running front middle to rear corner of cab (*see* picture of 26040 on 31st May 1959 at Wath with 26049 and 26019) but also a small downward, front to back, straight sloping strip over the Driver and Secondman windows at 31st May 1959. Also 26033 at 21st March 1973: no square vent at the time!

(above, left) **76051 and 76008 stable at Rotherwood on 27th May 1981, waiting for the next westbound load. It will be noticed that the cab roof rain strips on these two now consist a curved strip on each side of the roof protecting the door and opening side window – nothing more!** ***Graham Jelly.*** *(above right)* **76023 and 76027, on rail tour duty at Dinting, show off their roof aspect on 13th October 1979.** ***Norman Preedy.*** *(below, left)* **Seen at Orgreave SP on 18th April 1981, 76009 had managed to retain its front rain strip on both cabs.** ***S.Carter.*** *(below, right)* **The raised eyebrows! Quite a few of the EM1s got this style at some period in their lives. No.26033 had that look on 21st March 1973 when photographed at Godley Junction.** ***Norman Preedy.***

ROLLER BEARING AXLEBOXES

Nos.26046 and 26048 to 26057 were built with Timken roller bearing axleboxes whilst other members of the class received them when bogie exchanges took place. Therefore, some of the locomotives numbered 26048 to 26057 reverted to the original type axlebox as fitted to 26000 to 26045 and 26047 as under.

Locomotives built with Timken Roller Bearing axleboxes:

26046
26048 up to 8/65>
26049
26050
26051 off by 4/69.
26052 off by 1956.
26053 off by 8/66.
26054 up to 4/69> off by 3/73.
26055 up to 1/61.
26056
26057 to at least 6/71.

The following locomotives gained Timken Roller-Bearing axleboxes through bogie exchange at various 'shoppings': 76003 by 3/74, 26004 by 10/55, 76008 by 3/74, 26011 by 9/73, 26016 23/2/69, 26017 by 6/57, 76020, 76023 by 10/76, 76024 by 3/77, 26026, 26027 before 3/74, 26035, 76040 by 3/77, 76041 by 3/74, 76047 by 8/74.

Whilst these changed or changed back to the original type axlebox through bogie exchange: 76004 by ?/?, 76047 by 4/78, 26048, 76050, 26051 by 4/69, 26052 by 1956, 26053 by 8/66, 26054 by 3/73, 76055 by 11/73, 26056, 76057.

76020 changed *back* to the original bogies prior to preservation.

Regained Timken axlebox bogies: 76052 by ?/?.

VENTILATION 'SLOTS'

During their lives the EM1s especially were subject to various experiments and implementations of extra means of ventilation. Not only was extra ventilation (in the form of slots and varying shapes of holes cut into the bodywork) required for the enclosed electrical apparatus but the cabs of both classes were subjected to condensation and draughts which called for various measures and remedies throughout the lifetime of the locomotives.

So far earliest horizontal slots were on: 26001, 26002, 26003, 26004, 26005, 26006, 26011, 26012, 26013, 26014, 26016, 26019, 26020, 26023, 26025, 26026, 26027, 26028, 26029, 26036, 26039, 26040, 26044, 26050, 26051, 26054, 26055, 26056 all, it seems, when new.

EM1 – Earliest cab square vents were on: 26005, 26011, 26018, 26024, 26038, 26041, 26047 – 7/10/62. None at 5/60 – 26011, 26018, 26044. None at 4/2/62 – 26002. Eventually all survivors were equipped.

EM2 – Earliest cab square vents were on: 27004 – 8/12/62. None at 14/6/61 – 27002. All so fitted, and then kept in Holland.

Earliest round vent louver over cab side windows: EM1 – 26019 undated (?/59) but in black livery; 26046, 26051 – 29/10/61; EM2 – 27000 – 7/59. None at 7/59 – 27005.

EM1 – Small moveable louver type ventilators above cab doors were fitted to 26025 and 26019 on 11th December 1968.

A retrofitted type of body ventilation, whereby five small elongated openings were cut out of the top of the second panel behind the Secondmans' door on the non-corridor side of the locomotives were carried out during the late 1970s to the following: 76007, 76008, 76010, 76011, 76016, 76021, 76024, 76025, 76030, 76031.
Not by: 21/3/73 – 76015, E26041, E26052, E26054;
Not by 19/3/74 – 76004, 76006, 76027, 76056;
Not by 21/8/74 – 76026, 76037, 76047;
Not by 30/3/77 – 76001, 76035, 76039, 76043, 76048.
Not by 14/10/78 – 76009;
Not 76023, 76027, 76052 – by 13/10/79;
Not by 27/4/80 – 76015, 76053;
Not by 14/6/81 – 76013.

WINDSCREEN WIPERS: Air operated windscreen wipers fitted to all EM1s from January 1957 onwards. Manual type beforehand.

WORKS PLATES
When new (to be more precise ex-Gorton but pre-Dukinfield and built might be a better description), Nos.26001 and 26002 did not at first carry works plates nor in fact any plates. Also,their fleet numbers were located much lower on the cab side sheet, about central with the top end of the vacuum hose connection coming out of the cab front panel. This seems to coincide with delivery to Dukinfield with no plates prior to fitting of the electrical components, including motors, and then the return to Gorton works fully equipped and ready for traffic when they were eventually fitted with both Gorton worksplates and Metropolitan-Vickers plates.

CLASS 77

WINDSCREEN WIPERS: All the class were fitted from new with conventional screen wipers (one for each window connected to a motor at the top of the screen).

ROTARY WINDSCREEN WIPERS

The naval-type windscreen wipers (clearers), as they were known to the MSW crews, used to get very dirty inside. The first one fitted, 1964, actually had the motor in the centre of the window on the drivers side which somewhat restricted vision! Only EM2 No.27002 was fitted – No.1 end cab – and there the experiment stopped for various reasons. The fitting of good quality powered wipers negated any further investigation into rain and snow clearance on the front windows.

RAIN STRIPS

The whole class appear to have been fitted early on with large continuous rain strips side to side, and receding, with front to rear strips over doorways. No changes have been noted.

(above) **Along with the rest of the EM1s and EM2ss, both EM1 No.E26024 and EM2 No.27006 had acquired the small square vent holes above each side window on both sides of the cabs by the mid 1960s.** ***Norman Preedy.***

(below) **Heading uphill through the Longdendale valley with a Manchester–Sheffield service during the latter stages of its BR life, blue-liveried 27002 shows off the naval-type rotary window 'wipers' which became more of a nuisance than an asset. When the first example was fitted, the motor which drove the wiper was located directly in the drivers' line of sight!** ***Transport Treasury.***

'LIVERY' CHANGES DURING 'TOPS' PERIOD

Key:
(1) Locomotive.
(2) Dates of observations with any changes.
(3) Position of BR double-arrow symbol U-upper; L-lower; BR -BR crest.
(4) Numbers - 4 in early period; 2 in later period [Some class members kept all four numbers].
(5) Number of Works Plates - 4, 2, 0. Metro-Vick plates were usually removed when the works plates were finally taken off.
(6) Position of the TOPS Information box - C centred over worksplate; R right of worksplate centre line but above.

(1)	(2)	(3)	(4)	(5)	(6)	***Notes***
76001	19/03/74	?	?	4	C	
76001	30/03/77	L	2	4	C	
76001	18/04/81	L	2	0	C	*Withdrawn*
76002	18/04/81	U	2	0	C	*Withdrawn.*
76003	06/11/69	L	4	3	R	*As E26003.*
76003	05/05/74	L	4	4	R	
76036	07/11/81	U	2	0	?	*Reno. 76036 from 10/76. Withdrawn Metro-Vick plate removed.*
76004	21/03/73	U	4	4	C	*As E26004.*
76004	19/03/74	U	2	4	C	
76006	21/08/74	L	2	4	R	*Metro-Vick plate removed.*
76006	07/06/78	L	2	0	R	
76006	04/03/81	L	2	0	?	
76007	16/03/77	U	2	4	R	
76007	25/04/81	U	2	0	C	
76008	18/05/69	L	4	3	R	*AS E26008.*
76008	19/03/74	U	2	0	C	*Number and Tops box set equal distance from upper and lower edges of cab side below window.*
76008	01/09/77	U	4	0	C	
76008	03/08/80	U	4	0	C	
76008	08/02/81	U	4	0	C	
76009	21/03/73	BR	4	4	R	*As E26009.*
76009	19/03/77	L	2	2	R	
76009	30/03/77	L	2	4	R	
76009	14/10/78	L	2	0	R	
76009	18/04/81	L	2	0	R	
76010	21/08/74	L	4	0	C	*Metro-Vick plate removed.*
76010	19/03/77	L	4	0	C	
76010	07/03/81	L	4	0	C	
76011	01/09/73	L	4	0	R	
76011	30/03/77	L	4	0	R	
76011	07/03/81	L	4	0	R	
76012	21/08/74	L	4	0	R	
76012	11/06/79	L	4	0	R	
76012	25/04/81	L	4	0	R	
76013	19/03/74	U	4	0	R	
76013	16/09/78	U	4	0	R	
76013	14/06/81	U	4	4	R	*Unusual to have any, never mind all four works plates and the Metro-Vick plates at this date. However, they appear to have been stored for some years and then re-affixed for some special event.*
76014	21/03/73	None	4	4	R	*As E26014. No BR crest either.*
76014	30/03/77	U	2	4	C	
76014	25/03/81	U	2	0	C	
76015	21/03/73	U	4	4	R	
76015	07/03/80	U	4	0	R	
76015	25/03/81	U	4	0	R	
76016	23/02/69	L	4	4	none	*As E26016.*
76016	19/03/77	L	—	—	—	
76016	14/10/78	L	4	0	?	
76016	09/01/81	L	4	0	R	
76018	21/03/73	U	4	4	R	*As E26018.*
76018	26/08/74	U	2	4	R	
76035	19/03/77	U	2	4	C	*Reno. 76035 from 6/76. All plates taken off by May 77.*
76035	15/10/77	U	2	0	C	*Ex works.*
76020	16/03/77	U	2	4	R	
76021	24/07/74	L	4	2	R	
76021	16/09/78	L	4	0	R	
76021	03/08/80	L	4	0	R	
76021	08/02/81	L	4	0	R	
76022	21/08/73	BR	4	2	R	
76022	12/10/76	BR	4	2	R	
76022	18/04/81	BR	4	0	C	
76023	12/10/76	L	4	4	C	
76023	16/03/77	L	4	4	C	
76023	13/10/79	L	4	0	C	
76023	04/03/81	L	4	0	C	
76024	21/03/73	L	4	4	C"	*As E26024. * Tops box on right hand cab side above the number. No Metro-Vick plate.*
76024	16/03/77	L	2	4	R	
76024	04/03/81	L	2	0	R	

During the TOPS period of their lives, the 76s (EM1s) underwent a surprising number of changes to their outward appearance; what might be termed as 'livery' for want of a better desccription. These changes encompassed numbers, positioning of numbers, positioning of TOPS boxes, the location of the BR double-arrow symbol (except in one extreme case), and removal of brassware. The accompanying table (pages 148 and 151) gives an indication of what was happening regarding the changes to each locomotive at different periods of their lives, although specific dates are given in most cases. Modellers will hopefully find the table of some use but it is by no means exhaustive in its scope and coverage.

76022 stabled at Guide Bridge on 21st March 1973. Having been one of the early recipients fitted for MU operations, this EM1 was virtually assured to operate to the end, and it did! However, by some measure of luck, deviousness by certain members of BR staff, and other factors, 76022 managed to keep its BR crest; not having to contend with the small version handed out to the named members of the class, the example carried by 76022 was a large version which you could not miss. Still to be renumbered E26029 is coupled but when it was renumbered in 1974 it lost its crest for the double arrow symbol. ***Norman Preedy.***

With the TOPS information box taking up much of the space formerly occupied by a worksplate, 76023 has nothing other than two redundant bolts filling the holes where the flat headed screws secured the worksplate. The information now reveals a total weight of 89 tons against the original 86 tons 14 hundredweight. Should that be tonnes or was something 'extra' fitted to the insides of the EM1s? The prototype, 26000, weighed in at 89 tons exactly in working order whereas the production batch tipped the scales at just below 87 tons. Even those fitted with train heating boilers only ever weighed 87 tons 6 hundredweight! So, the TOPS box is somewhat ambiguous perhaps? ***Hugh P.Searle.***

In the sidings on the west side of Reddish depot, on a damp Saturday 6th November 1976, smartly turned-out 76003 heads a line-up consisting sisters 76055, 76035, and BR Sulzer Type 2 diesels 24024 and 24021. Only the day before, 76003 had returned from a major overhaul at Crewe hence the fresh coat of paint. However, 76003 was in fact 76036 in disguise, renumbered during the period in 1976 when efforts were made to 'tidy-up' the class numbering. At the same time, 76036 became 76003! Within twelve months our subject here would have paid another visit to Crewe to have air brakes and multiple unit equipment fitted for working the MGR coal trains over the MSW. The vacuum brake with its prominent hose was removed at the same 1977 works visit. ***Hugh P.Searle.***

(above) **Long term storage at Reddish 2nd August 1977! 76055 and 76050 have by now had their pantographs removed. Even the sand box lids have been taken off. The numbers, symbols and boxes still stand out against the overpowering BR blue livery. Although not important, it is interesting to note that all the locomotives in view have all got the same equipment room side showing to the camera – such uniformity was a rarity after thirty-odd years of service. In the foreground is the track which was formerly used to stable diesel multiple units when they were refuelled and when Reddish had the responsibility for looking after the Derby Lightweight units which once worked out of London Road station over the ex-Great Central lines in south-east Manchester.** ***Hugh P.Searle.***

(left) **Just in case you need to know where the BR crest was located – 76022 at Guide Bridge 18th April 1981 with the only example which survived to the end.** ***S.Carter.***

76025	28/03/75	U	4	0	?	
76025	14/07/77	U	2	2	C	
76025	26/03/81	U	2	0	C	
76026	c1972	L	4	4	R	*As E26026.*
76026	21/08/74	U	2	4	C	*Ex works.*
76026	16/03/77	U	2	2	C	
76026	11/12/79	U	2	0	C	
76027	19/03/74	L	2	4	R	
76027	16/03/77	?	2	4	R	
76027	13/10/79	U	2	0	R	
76027	26/02/81	U	2	0	C	
76028	21/03/73	BR	4	4	R	*As E26028.*
76028	15/10/77	L	2	0	R	
76028	26/02/81	L	2	0	R	
76029	15/10/77	?	?	0	C	
76029	05/05/79	U	2	0	C	
76030	01/01/73	L	4	4	R	*As E26030. MV plate fitted.*
76030	19/03/77	L	4	2	R	
76032	15/10/77	U	2	0	R	
76032	19/05/78	U	2	0	R	
76033	21/03/73	BR	4	3	R	*As 26033. No Metro-Vick plate!*
76033	15/10/77	U	2	0	R	
76034	00/06/79	U	2	0	R	
76034	18/04/81	U	2	0	R	
76036	19/03/74	U	4	4	C	
76003	18/04/81	U	2	0	C	*Reno. 76003 from 10/76. Withdrawn.*
76037	21/08/74	BR	4	4	R	*Fleet numbers in old style except for first '7' which was smaller.*
76037	30/03/77	U	2	4	R	*Numbers now in new style.*
76037	26/03/81	U	2	0	R	
76038	21/08/74	L	4	0	R	
76050	01/05/78	L	2	0	R	*Reno.76050 from 10/76. Withdrawn. Grounded.*
76039	21/03/73	L	4	4	C	*As E26039. No Metro-Vick plate.*
76039	19/03/74	U	2	4	C	*Fleet number not centre with works plate or Tops box.*
76048	16/03/77	U	2	4	C	*Reno. 76048 from 10/76. Metro-Vick plate removed.*
76040	21/08/74	U	2	4	C	
76040	16/03/77	U	2	2	R	*Worksplates removed from blank cab sides. No Metro-Vick plates.*
76040	02/06/78	U	2	0	R	
76040	21/03/80	U	2	0	R	
76041	21/03/73	L	4	4	C	*As E26041.*
76041	19/03/74	U	2	4	R	
76043	30/03/77	L	4	4	R	*No Metro-Vick plates.*
76043	18/04/81	L	4	0	R	*Withdrawn, Grounded.*
76044	—	—	—	—	—	
76031	16/03/77	U	2	4	C	*Reno. 76031 from 3/76.*
76031	15/10/77	U	2	0	C	
76031	18/04/81	U	2	0	C	
76046	05/04/69	L	4	4	?	*As E26046. Name still carried.*
76046	21/03/73	L	4	2	R	*As 26046. No Metro-Vick plate.*
76046	30/03/77	L	2	2	C	
76046	12/08/79	L	2	0	C	*Metro-Vick plate removed.*
76047	21/08/74	U	2	4	R	*Metro-Vick plate in situ.*
76047	15/04/78	U	2	0	R	
76048	21/03/73	L	4	4	R	
76048	21/08/74	L	4	4	R	*Metro-Vick plates in situ.*
76039	30/03/77	L	2	4	R	*Reno. 76039 from 10/76.*
76039	23/04/81	U	2	0	none	
76049	21/03/73	U	4	4	C	
76049	26/08/74	U	4	4	C	
76049	08/08/78	L	2	0	?	
76050	14/03/70	BR	4	4	R	*As E26050. No name plate.*
76050	22/03/73	U	4	4	R	*Metro-Vick plate in situ.*
76038	08/02/80	U	2	0	R	*Reno. 76038 from 11/76.*
76051	08/04/69	BR	4	4	none	*As E26051. No nameplates carried.*
76051	01/06/69	BR	4	4	R	*As E26051. No name.*
76051	18/04/81	L	2	0	C	*Metro-Vick plate also removed.*
76052	21/03/73	U	4	3	C	*As E26052.*
76052	19/03/77	U	2	0	C	*Metro-Vick plate removed.*
76052	20/05/79	U	2	0	C	*Withdrawn*
76053	27/04/80	U	2	0	C	*Metro-Vick plate removed.*
76053	18/04/81	U	2	0	C	*Withdrawn.*
76054	08/04/69	BR	4	4	R	*As E26054 narrow figures. Nameplates attached.*
76054	21/03/73	L*	4	4	none	*As E26054 (modern figures used). * Nameplate recently removed.*
76054	22/09/74	L	2	4	?	*Metro-Vick plate in situ.*
76054	18/04/81	L	2	0	none	*Metro-Vick plate also removed.*
76055	30/03/77	U	2	0	C	*Withdrawn. Metro-Vick plate also removed.*
76056	21/03/73	U	4	4	C	*As E26056.*
76056	19/03/74	U	2	4	C	*Metro-Vick plate in situ.*
76056	30/03/77	U	2	4	C	*Metro-Vick plate removed.*
76056	18/04/81	U	2	0	C	*Withdrawn, Grounded.*
76057	02/05/71	L	4	4	R	*As E26057. Name removed.*
76057	21/08/74	L	4	4	?	*Number styles were as at withdrawal.*
76057	30/03/77	L	4	4	R	
76057	18/04/81	L	4	0	R	*First '7' later style, '6057' earlier style on all four cab-sides.. Withdrawn, Grounded.*

EXHIBITIONS & EXHIBITIONISTS

Both classes of MSW electric locomotives attended exhibitions over the years and one EM1 in particular became something of a celebrity. Others had their moments of glory and simply passed into history afterwards. However, 26020 made a habit of being in the right place or doing the right thing, at the right time. Such persistence earned it not only a place in history but also a life in preservation.

Exhibition attendees:

26020 Festival of Britain 1951.
26014 York Old station June 1951.
26020 Doncaster Works Centenary September 1953.
27002 Willesden exhibition 18th May to 10th June 1954.
27000 Rochdale 6th October 1956.
26026 Blast Lane goods depot, Sheffield 18th June 1958. EM1 was ex works! Others attending were: D201, D3063, a DMU, and BR Standard 9F No.92192
26013 Lincoln Holmes Exhibition 16th January 1959. In aid of the opening of the new goods shed! New diesel locomotives D5309, D3630, D2027 and six steam locomotives including A4 No.60022 were also in attendance. All, under cover.
E26013 Crewe Electric Depot Open Day, 19th April 1970.
76054 Barrow Hill Roundhouse Open Day 22nd September 1974.
76033 Tinsley Diesel Depot Open Day, 15th June 1980 (Centenary of ASLEF).

Preserved:

26020 NRM perpetual.
27000 Midland Railway Centre, Butterley.
27002 Musuem of Science & Industry, Manchester.

76039 No.1 end Cab only. MofS&I, Manchester.

(opposite, top) **26020 was not the only EM1 to claim exhibition status! During the Festival of Britain in 1951 a series of mini Festival of Britain exhibitions were held around the country to show off the best of British to those of the populace who could not make the trip to London. York was one such venue and from Monday 4th to Saturday 16th June the former railway station inside the city walls played host to a collection of locomotives and rolling stock. This view shows the exhibition gathered on the two tracks alongside the former station with the North Eastern Region headquarters, in the background, seemingly presiding over the event. Besides the obvious well known attractions – BRITANNIA, MALLARD, LOCOMOTION, and GNR Atlantic No.251 - an EM1 electric locomotive from the as yet to be completed MSW route was also invited to attend. Second locomotive in line, and tucked in behind No.70000, was No.26014. Sister No.26020 was of course down at the South Bank 'do' getting all the accolades there but 26014 was pristine enough for what was probably its only ever exhibition. *J. W.Armstrong (ARPT).***

(opposite, lower) **For the Centennial celebrations at Doncaster Locomotive Works in September 1953, EM1 No.26020 – what else – was invited along to join the party. Looking very smart, the EM1 was obviously making an impression on the public of the day and a walk through from cab-to-cab via the internal passageway was permitted. Note the lack of any train heating connection at this time. *Transport Treasury.***

76054 attended an open day at Barrow Hill depot on 22nd September 1974. It was neither totally cleaned or polished for the event but somebody had taken the trouble to paint the handrails in white and give the bufferbeam a lick of paint – 27002's external appearance at another roundhouse twenty-odd years beforehand was a completely different affair although Barrow Hill shed could rival 1A's shed for cleanliness. 76054 lasted until the very end of the MSW line but on two occasions it went into storage – serviceable – only to be re-instated, the sole member of the class to brush so closely with fate and get away with it twice. *Norman Preedy.*

26020

This is how 27002 was presented to that Willesden exhibition which was held in the roundhouse at the motive power depot. The date is 26th May 1954, some eight days after the start of the exhibition which ran until 10th June. Note that the building is extremely clean in every aspect; with over a quarter of a century of smoke and muck to remove or 'cover', I wonder how long it took the various parties to spruce the place up prior to the event. *Transport Treasury.*

Hardly an exhibition nor a display of capable vehicles. However, further down this line of discarded stock at Reddish depot on 2nd August 1977 is preservation candidate 76020. Attached to a brake van, the EM1 Bo+Bo is cleaned, polished and waiting for haulage to Doncaster where it will be got ready for permanent display at the National Railway Museum in York. No.76020 travelled within the 0730 Arpley-Doncaster freight on 10th August 1977. With 26000 Tommy but a memory by this time, 26020 seemed to be the most appropriate member of the class for preservation. *Hugh P.Searle.*

NAMES - EM1 & EM2

The names bestowed on the EM1s were removed after the passenger services ceased in January 1970 although some had been taken off beforehand.

Locomotive	***Name***	***Date***	***Naming Venue***	***Removed***
26000	TOMMY	30/6/52	Liverpool St. stn.	by 2/2/68 + worksplates.
26046	ARCHIMEDES	2/5/59	Gorton Wks.	
26047	DOIMEDES	13/9/60	Gorton Wks.	
26048	HECTOR	30/3/60	Gorton Wks.	
26049	JASON	23/8/60	Gorton Wks.	
26050	STENTOR	8/8/60	Gorton Wks.	
26051	MENTOR	23/6/59	Gorton Wks.	by 1/6/69.
26052	NESTOR	16/8/61	Gorton Wks.	
26053	PERSEUS	5/10/60	Gorton Wks.	
26054	PLUTO	8/4/61	Gorton Wks.	by 21/3/73.
26055	PROMETHEUS	8/6/59	Gorton Wks.	
26056	TRITON	1/7/59	Gorton Wks.	
26057	ULYSSES	11/4/60	Gorton Wks.	by 2/5/71.
27000	ELECTRA	17/8/59	Gorton Wks.	by 2/2/68 + worksplates.
27001	ARIADNE	29/9/59	Gorton Wks.	ditto
27002	AURORA	25/6/59	Gorton Wks.	ditto
27003	DIANA	10/1/61	Gorton Wks.	ditto
27004	JUNO	17/6/59	Gorton Wks.	ditto
27005	MINERVA	29/5/59	Gorton Wks.	ditto
27006	PANDORA	9/5/59	Gorton Wks.	ditto

A selection of nameplates carried by EM1s and EM2s. *(right)* **A close-up of the nameplate now carried by NS 1505 in preservation: Were these the original plates or replicas? Most of the original nameplates had been sold to private buyers by BR shortly after the seven Co-Co EM2s migrated to mainland Europe.** ***Hugh P.Searle.***

ACCIDENTS

For a class with such a small number of locomotives, working over a fairly short stretch of railway – albeit with a few steep and long grades – the EM1s certainly had their share of accidents and incidents. In the latter half of 1954 for instance no less than ten westbound goods trains got out of control on the descent from Woodhead but no all of those incidents resulted in accidents or damage. In 1955 a number of experiments were carried out and of a result of which all of the production batch of EM1s – 26001-26057 – were fitted with rheostatic braking which could be used to control the 850-ton mineral trains below 16 m.p.h. lower limit of the regenerative braking. Of the EM2 I have been unable to unearth any reported incidents but their even smaller number, and the fact that they rarely entered some of the yards which the EM1s frequented, would no doubt lessen their chances of being involved in the minor scrapes and derailments experienced by their smaller cousins. The following list is by no means exhaustive and, from what I have managed to find, there was possibly an equal number of incidents which were not reported. The list is in numerical order rather than chronological.

26001 – 1952 GE Lines – required works attention at Stratford for accident damage prior to returning to MSW line in November 1952.

26004 – March 1956, Torside crossing – Runaway and derailed whilst hauling westbound freight: bogie and cab damage.

76010 – December 1976, Mottram yard – Derailed at east end of yard whilst in charge of a loaded MGR. Wagons also derailed. Other engine of this working, the leading one, is unknown.

26017 – June 1957, Mottram – Derailed at Mottram yard.

E26017 – 19th February 1970, Sheffield – Involved in a mishap which resulted in a cab being damaged. It was condemned the following month at Reddish depot and cut up on site by contractors during October 1971. Seems to have been unlucky this one!

26019 – August 1954, Torside – Derailed at Torside Down Goods loop after being unable to stop in time whilst hauling a west-bound (down grade) loose-coupled freight. The locomotive managed to get through the gap between a footbridge support and overhead catenary support but hit the bufferstops and cab damaged. As a result of this and similar incidents, the EM1 class (excepting No.26000) were fitted with rheostatic braking to supplement the air brake. The regenerative braking system, which was fitted from new, was only effective above 16 m.p.h. so for adverse slow-speed circumstances the rheostatic system became normal.

E26022 – 2nd September 1971, Wentworth Junction – With E26025. Both locomotives damaged necessitating a visit to Crewe works for inspection.

26025 – August 1954, unknown location. Damage unknown but locomotive attended Gorton works for repairs.

26025 – *See* E26022 above.

76025 & **76027** – 8th April 1981, Hadfield – Some bogies of an eastbound anhydrous ammonia train derailed here. Locomotivs not damaged.

E26031 – Unknown date and location but withdrawn as a result and cut up at Crewe 1972.

26035 – August 1954, unknown location. Locomotive required new bogies because of collision damage.

26040 – March 1957, Torside crossing – Runaway and derailed with westbound coal train.

26047 – 1959, Nunnery sidings – Derailed when light engine.

26053 – 18th August 1967, Mottram yard – After running away with its train of thirty-two loaded coal wagons from Valehouse, and after being deliberately routed into Mottram yard in the hope that control could be regained, the EM1 was derailed by trap points at the west end of Mottram yard leading onto the main line. A third of the train was also derailed.

26th April 1978, Penistone – A pair of 76's (numbers unknown but 76034's No.1 end was damaged at about this time, including pantograph) were derailed at Huddersfield Jct. whilst working an MGR train.

76003 - 15th January 1980, Guide Bridge – En route to Reddish depot at 1900 hrs, the 76 had just passed through Guide Bridge station when it was sent down the non-electrified Stockport branch (apparently mistaken by the signalman for another train). Inevitably, even at the moderate speed of its passage, 76003 ran out of 'overhead' with the pantographs being tangled and then bringing down the wires, thus preventing the workings of the electric railway at least. Local services to and from Hadfield were then put into the hands of diesel multiple units. Later that day, when normality was restored at the western end of Guide Bridge station, **76051** managed to derail itself at Dewsnap sidings and eventually assistance was given by the Newton Heath breakdown train because the Longsight breakdown train was unavailable.

10th March 1981, Dinting station – Going out with a bang! Might be an appropriate description of the final months of the electrified Woodhead route. On this day a Godley to Tinsley mixed freight was wrecked just east of Dinting station when the fourth wagon of the train derailed west of the viaduct and which shortly afterwards started a chain of events culminating in all of the train, except the two locomotives (76028 and 76029), being strewn about the railway for a fair distance. Single line working remained in force for some days and was still taking place when another derailment occurred during the early hours of 8th April at a crossover at the western end of Hadfield station. The train concerned, from Runcorn to Immingham (locomotives 76025 and 76027), was made up of ammonia tanks and although eight of the bogie tanks had already negotiated the crossover safely, the ninth wagon derailed and continued on until it hit the platform at the station and overturned! Other wagons also became derailed and eventually two breakdown cranes (from Longsight and Tinsley depots) were required to clear the wreckage.

Besides the above listed accidents, at least three EM1s were condemned as a result of electrical problems and massive internal damage. Nos.**26035** and **26042** were both stored at Reddish from 22nd August 1968 after sustaining damage to their high tension compartments. Whether the similar incidents were related is unknown but it appears plausible that they were. Both engines were withdrawn in March 1970. Another with H.T. compartment damage was No.**26045** which was condemned on 29th November 1971. Although no incident has been traced to the contrary, **76056** ended up 'grounded' at Reddish and had a large 'bump' in its roof which was probably the reason for its demise.

EM1 No.26004 in trouble at Torside on 17th March 1956. It was not the only Bo+Bo to overrun the buffers at this place whilst working heavy Down coal trains unaided, and developing brake problems. Miraculously, the footbridge and the catenary survived the three known incidents. 26004 was eventually hauled out of its dilemma and sent to Gorton for attention. In the event it turned out that a Casual Heavy repair was required and the EM1 was in the shops until mid-September. ***Norman Preedy.*** *(below)* **Broken and shaken due to a derailment! 76034 which, on the day, was in the company of an unidentified sister working an MGR. train, was derailed at Penistone in April 1978. Although a bad time for any of the class to sustain accident damage, 76034 managed to survive withdrawal because of the recent expenditure in equipping the Bo+Bo with multiple unit and air brake components. Also, BR had only modified enough of the class to just about see through the MGR. workings. So, 76034 was repaired and thrust back out into traffic to work until the end. Note the missing pantograph in this view at Reddish on 2nd July 1978. Replacement windows, handrails, steps and even pantographs were all available – just!** ***Hugh P.Searle.***

SCRAPPING CHRONOLOGY - A Taster, and then The End: The Where, When, and how they got there!

1971:

October: It was reported that 26035 and 26042 were to be cut up at Reddish depot by J.Cashmore's of Great Bridge (known in their locale of the West Midland's as 'Honest John Cashmore' this firm became well known amongst railway enthusiasts nationwide when it became responsible for cutting up hundreds of steam locomotives during the great cull of the 1960s) after the same firm had dismantled 26017 during week ending. 9th October 1971.

1977:

76048 stored Reddish 27/3/77. Pantographs removed by 17/8/77.
76050 stored Reddish 27/3/77. Pantographs removed by 17/8/77. Grounded by 5/11/78.
76055 stored Reddish 27/3/77. Pantographs removed by 17/8/77.
76056 stored Reddish. Considerable accident damage to mid-roof and bodyside. Grounded by 5/11/78.
76057 stored Reddish 27/3/77. Pantographs removed by 17/8/77. Grounded by 5/11/78.

1983:

February: Staff from C.F.Booth of Rotherham started to cut up 76057 at the beginning of the month and by Saturday 12th it had been obliterated and a start was made on 76056 which had gone the same way by Saturday 19th!
The other two bodies, 76043 and 76050, were both full of asbestos and had to be moved from the depot yard to a suitable location and bogies were required for that process. Other asbestos fitted members of the class were 76002, 76004, 76048, 76052, and 76055 which were unsold during the initial tendering period.
Nos.76003, 76037, 76040 were sold to Vic Berry at Leicester (who had facilities for dealing with asbestos but apparently nonetheless declined to tender).
Nos.76029, 76031, 76032 and 76033 were sold to Coopers Metals, of Brightside, Sheffield.
C.F.Booth purchased the rest from Reddish.

Friday 25th February: 76015, 76041, 76046, 76049, 76053 departed Reddish as 9X43 the 1005 Reddish–Tinsley freight hauled by 40170 for C.F.Booth, Rotherham.

Tuesday 1st March: Reddish depot: 76043 and 76050 were both lifted onto salvaged bogies by the Crewe breakdown crane. Both 'complete' locomotives were then taken inside the shed to await further developments.

Saturday 5th March: C.F.Booth's yard at Rotherham: 76015, 76041, 76046, 76049 and 76053 were still intact. However, by Saturday 12th March only 76015 was still complete; 76041 had just the two burnt-out cabs remaining, 76053 also two cabs only, whilst 76046 was down to its frames with the cabs intact but off its bogies. 76049, which was also down to its frame, with control and electrical gear intact, was still on its bogies but being worked on!

Thursday 10th March: 76025, 76027, 76030, 76034, 76051 left Reddish as 9X31 the 1005 Reddish–Tinsley freight hauled by 47207 for C.F.Booth, Rotherham.
Wednesday 16th March: Nos.76029, 76031, 76032, and 76033 departed Reddish as 9X32 the 1005 Reddish–Sheffield Freight Terminal hauled by 47338, eventually destined for Coopers Metals, Brightside. The cavalcade actually stabled at Tinsley until Friday 18th when they were taken into Coopers yard.

Saturday 19th March: C.F.Booth's yard: 76041, 76046, 76053 had been cut up completely; 76015 frame cut up and two burnt-out cabs only; 76049 two cabs only. 76025, 76027, 76030, 76034, 76051 all intact.

(below) **As 76057 was being taken to pieces inside Reddish depot during July 1978, sister 76056 was awaiting its turn outside. Already written off due to accident damage, 76056 has also be subjected to vandalism of the unofficial kind.** ***Hugh P.Searle.***

CLASS EM1 (Class 76). Scrapping Summary.

26000 – :	Cut up at Crewe Works, 11/72.
26001 – 76001:	Cut up C.F.Booth, Rotherham, 5/83.
26002 – 76002:	Cut up C.F.Booth, Rotherham, 12/83.
26003 – 76003 – 76036:	Cut up C.F.Booth, Rotherham, 5/83.
26004 – 76004:	Cut up C.F.Booth, Rotherham, 1/84.
26005 – :	Cut up at Crewe Works, 6/71.
26006 – 76006:	Cut up C.F.Booth, Rotherham, 5/83.
26007 – 76007:	Cut up C.F.Booth, Rotherham, 6/83.
26008 – 76008:	Cut up C.F.Booth, Rotherham, 6/83.
26009 – 76009:	Cut up C.F.Booth, Rotherham, 7/83.
26010 – 76010:	Cut up C.F.Booth, Rotherham, 6/83.
26011 – 76011:	Cut up C.F.Booth, Rotherham, 6/83.
26012 – 76012:	Cut up C.F.Booth, Rotherham, 7/83.
26013 – 76013:	Cut up C.F.Booth, Rotherham, 5/83.
26014 – 76014:	Cut up C.F.Booth, Rotherham, 5/83.
26015 – 76015:	Cut up C.F.Booth, Rotherham, 3/83.
26016 – 76016:	Cut up C.F.Booth, Rotherham, 4/83.
26017 – :	Cut up at Reddish depot by J.Cashmore, Great Bridge, w/e 9/10/71.
26018 – 76018 – 76035:	Cut up C.F.Booth, Rotherham, 6/83.
26019 – :	Cut up at Crewe Works, 4/72.
26020 – 76020:	Sent Reddish to Doncaster Works 10/8/77 for repainting prior to display at NRM York.
26021 – 76021:	Cut up C.F.Booth, Rotherham, 3/83.
26022 – 76022:	Cut up C.F.Booth, Rotherham, 5/83.
26023 – 76023:	Cut up C.F.Booth, Rotherham, 4/83.
26024 – 76024:	Cut up C.F.Booth, Rotherham, 6/83.
26025 – 76025:	Cut up C.F.Booth, Rotherham, 3/83.
26026 – 76026:	Cut up C.F.Booth, Rotherham, 7/83.
26027 – 76027:	Cut up C.F.Booth, Rotherham, 3/83.
26028 – 76028:	Cut up C.F.Booth, Rotherham, 6/83.
26029 – 76029:	Cut up Coopers Metals, Brightside, 3/83.
26030 – 76030:	Cut up C.F.Booth, Rotherham, 4/83.
26031 – :	Cut up at Crewe Works, 5/72.
26032 – 76032:	Cut up Coopers Metals, Brightside, 3/83.
26033 – 76033:	Cut up Coopers Metals, Brightside, 3/83.
26034 – 76034:	Cut up C.F.Booth, Rotherham, 3/83.
26035 – :	Cut up at Reddish depot by J.Cashmore, Great Bridge, 10/71.
26036 – 76036 – 76003:	Cut up Vic Berry, Leicester, 5/83.
26037 – 76037:	Cut up Vic Berry, Leicester, 4/83.
26038 – 76038 – 76050:	Cut up C.F.Booth, Rotherham, 2/84.
26039 – 76039 – 76048:	Cut up C.F.Booth, Rotherham, 2/84.
26040 – 76040:	Cut up Vic Berry, Leicester, 5/83.
26041 – 76041:	Cut up C.F.Booth, Rotherham, 3/83.
26042 – :	Cut up at Reddish depot by J.Cashmore, Great Bridge, 10/71.
26043 – 76043:	Cut up C.F.Booth, Rotherham, 2/84.
26044 – 76044 – 76031:	Cut up Coopers Metal, Brightside, 2/84.
26045 – :	Cut up at Crewe Works, 4/72.
26046 – 76046:	Cut up C.F.Booth, Rotherham, 3/83.
26047 – 76047:	Cut up C.F.Booth, Rotherham, 5/83.
26048 – 76048 – 76039:	Cut up C.F.Booth, Rotherham, 6/83. Before disposal, the No.1 end cab was removed at Reddish depot and preserved at MMofS&I as 76039.
26049 – 76049:	Cut up C.F.Booth, Rotherham, 3/83.
26050 – 76050 – 76038:	Cut up C.F.Booth, Rotherham, 5/83.
26051 – 76051:	Cut up C.F.Booth, Rotherham, 3/83.
26052 – 76052:	Cut up C.F.Booth, Rotherham, 2/84.
26053 – 76053:	Cut up C.F.Booth, Rotherham, 3/83.
26054 – 76054:	Cut up C.F.Booth, Rotherham, 5/83.
26055 – 76055:	Cut up C.F.Booth, Rotherham, 2/84.
26056 – 76056:	Cut up at Reddish depot by C.F.Booth, 3/83.
26057 – 76057:	Cut up at Reddish depot by C.F.Booth, 3/83.

76050 has been grounded good and proper in this 2nd July 1978 view of the area located just east of the servicing shed where the Glossop units stabled. The exact date of grounding has been lost in time but this image reveals the near permanence of the predicament exacted on 76050. ***Hugh P.Searle.***

(above) **The corridor of grounded 76050 on 2nd July 1978! Although not revealing a complete and intact locomotive, this interior view allows us to take in the construction of the body with the various compartments located on the right. On the floor on the immediate right can be seen the large ballast weight fitted to locomotives not equipped with train heating boilers.** ***Hugh P.Searle.***

(centre right) **Reddish depot, April 1983: The EM1s have been sorted into the groups which would make the final journeys together into oblivion. This view of 76010 and 76037 presents two contrasting front ends insofar that the latter had lost its dual brake status some years beforehand whereas 76010 managed to keep the vacuum brake to the end. The various groups which travelled to the scrapyards together are listed elsewhere in this chapter but these two certainly ended up at different yards and, some distance apart too!** ***Hugh P. Searle.***

Perhaps the ending at Reddish was more like an evacuation than a 'clearing-out' although some of the asbestos affected locomotives were kept behind after that Spring clear-up of 1983 simply because a buyer, who could handle their disposal safely, had to be found. In April 1983 76004 was one of the 'asbestos lot' and which were easily identified because they were all vacuum brake only machines. Here in the sidings on the west side of the depot the Bo+Bo looks decidedly unwanted. ***Hugh P.Searle.***

cont./ from page 158.
Saturday 19th March: Cooper's Metals yard, Brightside: 76029, 76031, 76032, 76033 all intact.

Thursday 24th March: Nos.76007, 76011, 76022, 76024, and 76035 left Reddish as 9X14 the 1005 Reddish–Tinsley freight hauled by 40168 for C.F.Booth, Rotherham.

Saturday 26th March: Cooper's Metals: 76029 had lost its roof and most internal equipment.

Tuesday 29th March: Nos.76012, 76016, 76021, 76023, 76026 went as 9X53 the 1005 Reddish–Tinsley freight, hauled by 37130. Destined for C.F.Booth, Rotherham.

Thursday 31st March: C.F.Booth's yard: 76034 had been cut up whilst 76027 and 76030 were nearly so. The other eleven – 76007, 76011, 76012, 76016, 76021, 76022, 76023, 76024, 76026, 76035, 76051 – remained intact.

Thursday 31st March: Cooper's Metals yard: 76031, 76032 intact. 76029 (one cab) and 76033 (both cabs) were down to frames although still on their bogies.

Wednesday 13th April: Nos.76001, 76008, 76009, 76028, and 76036 departed from Reddish as 9X26 the 1005 Reddish–Tinsley freight hauled by 40056 destined for C.F.Booth, Rotherham. This train was delayed at Earles sidings on the Hope Valley line when No.76036 developed a hot-box and had to be detached and left at the sidings.

(opposite, bottom) **After giving up its No.1 end cab to the Manchester Museum of Science & Industry, 76039 was treated just like the others – as a lump of scrap metal. However, 76039 was not going to Rotherham without a fight; well, wouldn't you!?** ***Hugh P.Searle.***

Thursday 14th April: Nos.76003, 76037, and 76040 left Reddish depot as 9X25 Reddish–Leicester Humberstone Road freight hauled by 37193 destined for V.F.Berry, Leicester.

Friday 15th April: C.F.Booth's yard: 76016, 76027, 76030 had been cut up, 76051 was being cut up. Others intact.

Friday 15th April: Cooper's Metals yard: 76029, 76032, 76033 had been cut up completely, whilst 76031 was totally intact.

Wednesday 20th April: Nos.76006, 76013, 76014, 76038, and 76047 left Reddish as 9X50 the 1005 Reddish–Tinsley freight hauled by 40056 destined for C.F.Booth, Rotherham. This particular train was also delayed at Earles siding when 76013 had to be detached with a hot-box. Note the motive power!

Saturday 23rd April: C.F.Booth's yard: 76051 comprised two burnt-out cabs whilst 76001 and 76021 were being broken up.
Saturday 23rd April: Vic Berry's yard, Braunstone Gate, Leicester: 76003 was intact whilst 76037 and 76040 were both being broken up.

Tuesday 26th April: C.F.Booth's yard: 76015, 76025 and 76049 were gone!

Wednesday 27th April: Nos.76010, 76039, and 76054 departed from Reddish as 9X86 the 1005 Reddish–Tinsley freight hauled by 37265 for C.F.Booth, Rotherham. En route a stop was made at Earles sidings to attach 76013 and 76036 but 'one-cab' 76039 then had to be detached because it had run hot!

With the three departing Reddish on 27th April for Rotherham, seven 76's – all with asbestos clad cabs – remained unsold and were left inside the depot: 76002, 76004, 76043, 76048, 76050, 76052, 76055. The Manchester–Glossop electric multiple units (Class 506) were now visiting Longsight for maintenance and stabling, a power supply at

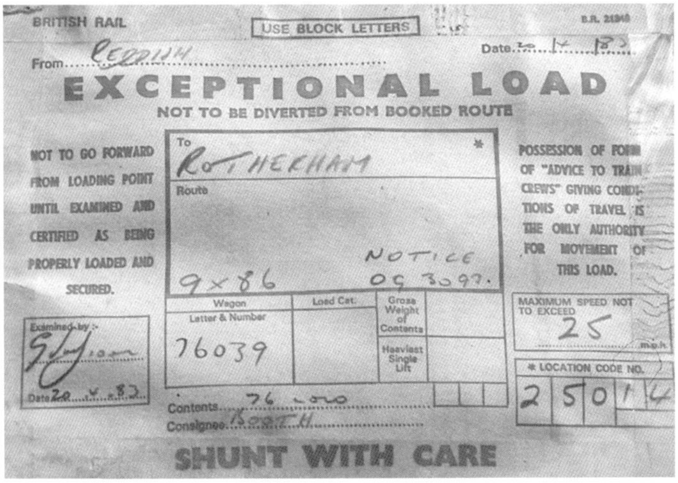
BRITISH RAIL
USE BLOCK LETTERS
B.R. 21940
From REDDISH
Date 20 / 4 / 83
EXCEPTIONAL LOAD
NOT TO BE DIVERTED FROM BOOKED ROUTE
NOT TO GO FORWARD FROM LOADING POINT UNTIL EXAMINED AND CERTIFIED AS BEING PROPERLY LOADED AND SECURED.
To ROTHERHAM *
Route
9X86 NOTICE OG 3097.
POSSESSION OF FORM OF "ADVICE TO TRAIN CREWS" GIVING CONDITIONS OF TRAVEL IS THE ONLY AUTHORITY FOR MOVEMENT OF THIS LOAD.
Examined by:-
Date 20 . 4 . 83

Wagon Letter & Number	Load Cat.	Gross Weight of Contents	
76039		Heaviest Single Lift	

MAXIMUM SPEED NOT TO EXCEED 25 m.p.h.
* LOCATION CODE NO. 2 5 0 1 4
Contents 76 LOCO
Consignee BOOTH
SHUNT WITH CARE

(top) **One-cab 76039 resides in the head shunt at Earles sidings on 30th April 1983. This wasn't the first of the class to run hot whilst en route from Manchester to Sheffield. On 13th April 76036 had to be detached from its special 9X26. A week later 76013 re-enacted the same scenario when it was taken out of train 9X50. When 76039 was being hauled east on 27th April in special 9X86, with 76010 and 76054, it too was detached and dumped at Earles. During the same shunting manoeuvre the two earlier miscreants, 76013 and 76036 were attached to the special for onward transit to Tinsley. On Wednesday 18th May 76039 resumed its melancholy final journey being the sole occupant of train 9X48 Earles-Tinsley freight. However, it would be another month before the former EM1 entered Booths yard in Rotherham. Misbehaviour by the doomed 76s did not end with 76039s departure from Earles. Later in the year, on Thursday 1st December, whilst part of Ashburys-Tinsley special 9X87, 76004 and 76055 both ran hot and once again Earles siding provided a temporary resting place. As it turned out, that pair became the last residents of the Hope valley refuge but they apparently displayed a further reluctance to journey onwards and did not leave that location until after Christmas. Note the accumulation of slimy filth on the roof of the locomotive; the bodyside is however rather smart, at least from this aspect.** ***Hugh P.Searle.*** *(above, left)* **The Exceptional Load notice attached – by adhesive tape – to 76039. This was stuck to the cab-side of the locomotive when it was recorded at Earles siding on 30th April. No consideration for the tape's treatment by the weather appears to have been made and already it is struggling to adhere to the painted surface. The notice was filled out on 20th April, a week earlier than the Bo+Bos journey began from Reddish in 9X86.** ***Hugh P.Searle.*** *(above, right)* **Page-out-of-a-notebook style notification indicating which of 76039's axleboxes was the culprit requiring attention at Earles siding.** ***Hugh P.Searle.***

(opposite, centre) **Another view of Booths yard in April 83'. Besides the seven 76s in view, a single item of London Transport underground stock inhabits the yard. From this aspect the yard appears very tidy. Three weeks earlier, on 31st March, it was reported that eleven of the class were intact in the yard. The situation changed daily however. with one or two locomotives being worked on until they ceased to exist.** *(opposite, bottom)* **Dual braked 76024 acquired bogies fitted with Timken axleboxes during its final decade. In this view at Booth's the distinctive covers have been removed, as have the bearings it seems (probably by souvenir hunters!) but that has revealed to us the view inside the axlebox which was somewhat different from the BR axleboxes. The axle nearest the camera, it will be noted, was smaller than the BR axles and appears to be slotted to allow the movement of oil. The bodyside at the other end of the locomotive has a 'square' cut which was not a sign that the scrap men had already started their task but was a cut made at Reddish to allow the easier removal of a compressor without resorting to removal of the roof panels; the panel was put back afterwards and secured in place by welded plates.** ***both Hugh P.Searle.***

76001 at Booths scrap yard in Rotherham on Sunday 17th April 1983. This pantograph-less Bo+Bo had departed from Reddish on Wednesday 13th April in the company of sisters 76008, 76009, 76028 and 76036 as special train 9X26 for Tinsley. En route 76036 developed a hot box and was detached at Earles sidings in the Hope valley to await attention; this was the first such incident involving the class during these special traffic movements. Note the rather smart condition of the locomotive behind (76008?), whilst on the ground adjacent to 76001 a pair of locomotive-less buffer heads remind us why these Bo+Bos are present in this yard. The stabling road had concrete sleepers which were less likely to catch fire during the dismantling process of locomotives and rolling stock when sparks from gas cutting gear could ignite wooden sleepers which were often soaked with oils and lubricants. 76001 had started to be broken up by Saturday 23rd April. ***Hugh P.Searle.***

(left) **E26031 outside the Motor traction Shop at Crewe on Sunday 23rd April 1972. Already condemned, the EM1 has lost its pantographs and would soon enter the shop to be dismantled to provide spares for the rest of the class. *Hugh P.Searle.***

(left, centre) **Remember that Danny Kaye song about a duck? This is 76043 hiding amongst the bushes and shrubs at Reddish, 18th April 1981. *S.Carter.***

cont./ from page 161.
Longsight being converted from a.c. to d.c. by 83009 acting as a generator.

Wednesday 18th May: 76039 resumed its journey to Booth's as 9X48 the 2014 Earles–Tinsley freight. Motive power unknown.

Saturday 11th June: C.F.Booth's yard: 76007, 76009, 76011, 76012, 76023, 76024, 76026, 76028, 76035 all intact. 76022 was off its bogies and consisted frame and cabs only. 76008 was off its bogies and had no cabs but had its power equipment compartment intact on the frame. 76010, off its bogies, had some power equipment and both cabs still on the frame. 76036 had been cut up since 29th May.

Wednesday 15th June: 76039 eventually arrived at Booth's after stabling in Tinsley yard since 18th May.

Sunday 19th June: C.F.Booth's yard: 76022 and 76036 had gone, whilst 76008 consisted just part of its frame only, 76010 and 76028 (off its bogies) were frames only. 76011 was being dismantled.

Thursday 24th November: Four of the 'asbestos seven' Nos.76002, 76043, 76048, 76050, which had been stabled at Ashburys for some time, left east Manchester as 9X38 the 1005 Ashburys–Tinsley freight hauled by 25221 for C.F.Booth, Rotherham.

Saturday 26th November: Cooper's Metals: 76031 still intact!

Thursday 1st December: The remaining members of the 'asbestos seven' Nos.76004, 76052, 76055 departed Ashburys as 9X87 the 1005 Ashburys–Tinsley freight hauled by 40044 for C.F.Booth, Rotherham. Earles sidings once again became a temporary stabling point for two of the 76s when both 76004 and 76055 were detached with hot boxes! 76052 was taken on to Rotherham by the Class 40.

One of the driving positions of 76024, though partially stripped in May 1983 at the Rotherham scrapyard, reveals the 1940s technology employed on the building and fitting out of these iconic locomotives. The lever 'stops' certainly did what it said on the tin! Note the photographer's adjustable spanner ready for dismantling horns; with the permission of C.F.Booth of course! *Hugh P.Searle.*

Sunday 4th December: C.F.Booth's yard: The five engines which arrived at the yard – 76002, 76043, 76048, 76050, 76052 – were still intact.

Sunday 18th December: Earles sidings, Hope Valley line: 76004 and 76055 were still resident on this date but had been moved by Friday 27th January 1984 (*see* below).

1984:

Sunday 15th January: Cooper's Metals: 76031, still intact but cutting up was completed by early February.

Sunday 29th January: C.F.Booth's yard: 76055 had just the two cabs to show of its former existence. 76002, 76043, 76048, 76050 were all still intact. 76004 and 76052 had been cut up.

Thursday 9th February: C.F.Booth's yard: 76002 one cab removed, dismantled internally and balanced on one intact bogie whilst the other was partly cut up. 76043 comprised just its cabs. 76048 consisted its frame only whilst 76050 was being opened up but was still on its bogies. 76055's remaining cab was being cut up.

Saturday 25th February 1984: C.F.Booth's yard: All evidence of Class 76 had gone!

(top) **During the mid to late Sixties' photographers around the country recorded mountains of steam locomotive scrap at a number of yards highlighting the sorry demise of the 'iron horse'. This is the equivalent hillock of electric locomotive 'bits' recorded by Hugh Searle at Booths scrapyard in Rotherham in April 1983. The bulk of the components appear to be the innards of traction motors which, if my maths is correct, amounted to 156 units in Booths case. Altogether the Class 76s broken up at C.F.Booths represented 3,393 tons of various scrap metals, give or take the odd missing pantograph, and cab!** *(centre)* **More 1940s 'technology' in the shape of the wheels used for the 76s! All of the large 'final drive' cogs attached to each axle seem to be well lubricated. After the non-ferrous components, the steel wheels and axles were amongst the choicest bits of ferrous scrap on the locomotives; high grade steel being a speciality of the area where the majority of the class met their end. This is a scene at Coopers Metals in Sheffield's Brightside district in April 1983. During that year Coopers acquired just four of the class, three being dealt with initially but the final one remaining intact until February 1984.** *(bottom)* **76031 at Coopers on 1st April 1983. It was virtually intact - virtually!** ***all Hugh P.Searle.***

Further into the yard at Booths in late April 1983 we come across both cabs of 76051 which were facing the same way! This was the main area of cutting-up with small manageable pieces of scrap mounting up behind ready for dumping into wagons or road vehicles for transit to the local steel plants or specialist metals companies. Stripping the electrical components must have been a mini industry by itself. Virtually intact 76021 looks on as if knowing that its turn for dismantling was imminent. Non-MU fitted 76051 left Reddish in train 9X31 on Thursday 10th March whilst 76021 departed from the erstwhile depot on Tuesday 29th March. By 23rd April both of these grounded cabs were burnt out whilst 76021 was being broken up. One of the floodlights at Rotherham United football ground can be seen in the left background. *Hugh P.Searle. (below)* Although a start was made in scrapping 76031 at Coopers in March 1983, it remained intact until February of the following year. Elements of Coopers main business at this time – cutting up wagons and passenger rolling stock – can be seen around the lone 76 in this view captured on 1st April 1983. *Hugh P.Searle.*

A broken back and a headache too! MU-fitted 76014 is all but finished at Booths yard during May 1983. The remaining central section of the relay and switch equipment still clinging to the frame of the locomotive would no doubt yield a fair amount of non-ferrous metals. On the ground one traction motor retains its casing and displays the axle groove to reveal where the motor was attached to the axle. Two other motor cores are ready for the pile seen earlier. *Hugh P.Searle.*

Three different shades of yellow warning paint adorn the ends of this trio of dual-braked 76s at Booths in May 1983. Left to right the weathering could be described by modellers as 'medium', 'light', and 'heavy'. 76008 was nearest. *Hugh P.Searle.*

Another painful view of 76014 during its final throes at the Rotherham yard! On the right is 76038 which arrived here in the same train as 76014 (9X50) in late April. Already a start has been made on the roof and body and within a few days 76038 will be in a similar state to 76014. *Hugh P.Searle.*

I have it on good advice that this is 76006, or at least part of it, in May 1983. Its two cabs are grounded and the twin bogies remain on the track alongside the ever diminishing hulk. Pipework apart, the two air storage tanks are the only recognisable bits of equipment remaining in this opened-out compartment. Booths employed a little diesel shunting locomotive at their Rotherham plant and its cab is just visible above the pile of scrap behind the bogie. *Hugh P.Searle.*

In amongst the mix! the remains of 76006 mingle with other unidentifiable pieces of metal at Booths in May 1983. Note the two diesel shunters hiding behind the piles. *(below)* **Even by 1983 educational standards were slipping but poetic emotions were still running high. 76043 cabside graffiti, Reddish depot, May 1983!** ***Hugh P.Searle.***

Amongst the last locomotives to reach the south Yorkshire scrapyards were the so-called 'Asbestos Seven' which were regarded, even in 1983, as something of a dangerous time bomb within our midst. Of course precautions were taken in handling and storing these members of the class which apparently had asbestos cladding within their cabs and bodies – 76002, 76004, 76043, 76048, 76050, 76052, and 76055 – and were unsold during the scrap tendering process of the class which had taken place after the fateful events of July 1981. Here, inside Reddish depot in May 1983, the seven 'dirty' and unsold locomotives headed by 76043, await further developments and negotiations between BR and invited scrap merchants. All seven have been boarded-up and secured to a fashion which in 1983 satisfied the relevant authorities. That the 'seven' were put under cover inside the depot was proof enough that the 'problem' was being taken seriously by all concerned. By the end of the year sales to C.F.Booth were secured and BR got rid of another of their asbestos problems. It would be interesting to know just how much CFB paid BR for the metal content of the locomotives. *(below)* **Except for the missing plates, 76043 was virtually complete when it was photographed outside the shed at Reddish in May 1983. This particular 76, along with the other 'dirty' locomotives, was a non air-braked example which had not been through the asbestos removal programme at Crewe like the air-braked and multiple unit members of the class had done. Note the green paint where the works plate was formerly located.** ***both Hugh P.Searle.***

A trio of 'dirty' 76s: 76004, 76055 and 76052 are stabled near the main road vehicle and pedestrian entrance to Reddish depot in April 1983. They were soon to be moved inside the shed and 'boarded-up' prior to completion of negotiations with Booth's, and the run-down of operations at the depot. Note the 'bashed face' of the Class 25 alongside with a 'not-to-be-moved' banner affixed. *Hugh P.Searle.*

All dressed up and nowhere to go! The 'Reddish Seven' inside the servicing shed at the Manchester depot in May 1983. Nowadays, because of the 'contaminated' occupants, this shed would be out of bounds to all except those dressed in appropriate protective suits, and with authorisation. The somewhat untidy nature of the shed says much about its future. Note the overhead wires have gone. *Hugh P.Searle.*

76043 again from a different angle. ***(below)*** **Judging by the amount of heavy rust around the axleboxes in June 1983, 76052 had lost its Timken covers long before it was corralled into the servicing shed at Reddish with the other six 'dirty' locomotives.** ***both Hugh P.Searle.***

The fact that BR required a consignment number for exceptional loads meant that the locomotive's own fleet number was convenient otherwise the numbers may well have been painted out as often happened with other items of rolling stock destined for scrap. 76055 is all this EM1 has left, its works plates long gone, even its TOPS box has disappeared whilst the paint finish is just that – finished! This was one of the pair which misbehaved whilst en route to Rotherham and had to be taken out of their special train at Earles siding, apparently spending Christmas 1983 at that location. Note the discarded EMU or DMU seat cushions on the floor. Reddish, June 1983. *Hugh P.Searle.*

76004 still displayed the 'footprint' of the first part of its original number with the E prefix some nine years after the TOPS number 7 was applied to the front of the final four digits. The paintwork is obviously much older than the renumbering, its faded glory, ex Crewe, was showing signs of rust breaking through whilst the roof was in an even worse state. The nearest bogie may well have been the one which caused 76004 to run hot when being towed for scrap in December 1983. Reddish, June 1983. *Hugh P.Searle.*

The oldest member of the 'Reddish Seven' and judging by appearances, the best kept, 76002 resides inside the shed at Reddish in June 1983. The Bo+Bo has acquired some new and rather novel axlebox covers – plywood – for its anticipated journey to the scrapyard. It was seemingly intended that nobody would gain entry into the cab prior to the locomotive being cut up but who controlled the handbrake release prior to departure from Reddish? *Hugh P.Searle.*

All seven of the 'dirty' 76s stabled inside Reddish depot in 1983 displayed different methods and levels of security to keep people out of their body shells. When did they all lose their pantographs and where did they go? *Hugh P.Searle.*

At the end of the line now of the seven asbestos 'wracked' 76s, we meet 76050 displaying its recently acquired bogies at Reddish depot in May 1983. 76050, along with 76043 had spent a considerable time grounded and to enable their eventual despatch to a suitable location where the asbestos problem could be dealt with, two sets of salvaged bogies were sought and each body was re-united with bogies. During the clearing of the depot site at Reddish in February 1983, grounded 76056 and 76057 were both cut up on site by staff from C.F.Booth. The same fate was in store for 76043 and 76050 but both were deemed to be too dangerous to tackle in the open-air and would instead require a specially adapted 'environment' in order to dismantle them safely. On Tuesday 1st March the Crewe breakdown crane was brought to the depot and it performed the task of lifting the errant bodies onto the respective bogies. Eventually the 'seven' vacated Reddish and were dumped in a siding on the Up side of the main line just east of Ashburys station. *(below)* **The southern end of Reddish depot in June 1983. Years of vandalism, even under the watchful eyes of a supposed security company, followed closure and by 1987 the place was deemed derelict and unwanted with the inevitable demolition taking place.** ***both Hugh P.Searle.***

Not quite closed for the last time! The southern end of the repair and lifting shop at Reddish in June 1983: The door on the right was fitted for the opening of the depot in 1954 but the door on the left was a much later fitting (I don't think the colour scheme had anything to do with age, dates, or history) which was eventually put in at some time after June 1959. Both doorways had been included in the design from the start but initially the left hand doorway was temporarily bricked-up, although the lintel and inside girder 'buttresses' were in place ready for the day when the opening-up took place. The track we see leading through in this view was a later extension of the original inside road which stopped short of this end by approximately one hundred yards! The overhead crane had two main hoists, each of 17.5 tons capacity, and an auxiliary hoist of five tons. The main job of the crane was to lift internal components and body parts of the locomotives, including whole pantograph sets; the latter directly to the first floor 'landing' featured in the illustration on page 68. The crane had been supplied by Stothert & Pitt Ltd., of Bath which might have seemed strange at the time because on the opposite side of the main line was another company – Whartons Cranes – which made and supplied similar machines worldwide. The 'can't miss' slogan adorning the crane had, by this date, been largely ignored but from its opening the authorities at Reddish had practised a 'good housekeeping' policy and every day normal work was stopped at a set time so that a clean-up could take place to keep the workshop clean and tidy. The official closing date for Reddish depot was 14th May 1983 after which a skeleton staff remained to clear certain items of equipment ready to mothball the depot for possible future use. The seven locomotives residing in the servicing shed were eventually moved to a siding just to the east of Ashburys station from where they would be taken away for scrap. *Hugh P.Searle.*

ON A LIGHTER NOTE!

There was once a green livery enhancing this EM1's bodywork but by 25th June 1964, when 26025 was photographed at Barnsley junction, Penistone, the paint had mainly turned to insipid shades grey. *David Christie.* *(below)* **Long before any of the class were fitted for MU working, Nos.26004 and 26005 double-head on Worsborough in August 1964. *Authors coll.***

On 1st June 1965 the Class leader runs into platform 2 at Sheffield (Victoria) having traversed the pointwork from platform 4. From here the Co-Co would run down to the western end of the platform and set back into the short siding (the Dock) alongside the hotel to await the next Down working. *Artc Slides.*

Departing from Piccadilly station, 27003 DIANA heads a Sheffield service on Thursday 25th June 1964. Even though it had only recently returned from Crewe, it managed to retain the lined green livery but had acquired the yellow warning panel. The combination of the maroon Mk.1 coaching stock and Brunswick green certainly made a statement. *David Christie.*

27006 stood outside the rebuilt Piccadilly station in Manchester on 1st June 1965. The EM2 is sporting the blue unlined (plain Jane) livery which was also applied to 27002. Note that on this non-corridor side of the body, the BR crest has been positioned on a raised rectangular plate located between the windows whereas on the corridor side it was applied directly to the bodywork (*see* 27000 for instance). Before the names were acquired, those which had the larger version of the new BR crest had it positioned on the lower section of the body, virtually centralised with the bogies on the non-corridor side (*see* also 27002) whilst on the other side it was put onto the upper section of the body between windows, above the third ventilator, in the same position where the old BR emblem had been located. *Artc Slides.* *(below)* **With one of the 'locals' admiring it, and before it was taken inside, NS 1505 (aka 27001) stands outside the main hall at the MMofS&I in Liverpool Road L&M station, basking in glorious 'Dutch' colours and preservation. *Hugh P.Searle.***

(above) **Vacuum fitted EM1, 76041 heads a line-up at Reddish on 2nd August 1977. MU fitted 76024 is 'inside' from 76041. Within this image not less than ten of the class are visible, which by this date consisted more than a fifth of the class. It might have been the Queen's Silver Jubilee year, but 1977 was to prove a bad year for Class 76 as further withdrawals and long term storage began. Reddish depot nevertheless continued to have a fairly high workload as more diesel locomotives arrived for attention. *Hugh P.Searle.***

AND FINALLY...

... A Modelling Slant on the MSW motive power.

The Woodhead line electric locomotives may be pure history, much like the line itself, but modellers nationwide have had a fascination of both the motive power and the railway which they served for some thirty years. One group of modellers in the East Midlands decided some decades ago to build a layout featuring a small section of the Manchester, Sheffield, Wath line and they based their model on Deepcar near Stocksbridge in Yorkshire. This particular location enabled them to run not just goods trains but passenger trains too.

I have been fortunate enough to have been acquainted with some of the members of this society and they have been kind enough to supply pictures of 'Deepcar' along with its locomotives, and a larger scale 'offshoot' known as Netherwood Sidings. So, below is a resume of Deepcar and a selection of images which show the evolution of railway modelling concerning the MSW as presented by the Nottingham Model Railway Society.

Deepcar – Nottingham Model Railway Society

Deepcar is a small town to the north-west of Sheffield. It was once served by the famous Manchester-Sheffield electrified main line, widely known as the 'Woodhead Route'. The Nottingham Model Railway Society has recreated the railway at Deepcar in 00 scale. The layout includes the exchange sidings for the nearby Stocksbridge steelworks as well as Deepcar Station and yard.

The model was started just a few years after the line closed (west of Deepcar) and at the time of writing is its now in its 24th year on the national exhibition scene. This layout is notable for featuring scratch-built near scale overhead electrification that actually works, and a fleet of iconic Class 76 electric locomotives (most kit-built) that draw power from it.

The overhead line equipment (OLE) was based on photographs and measurements of the de-energised equipment at Deepcar, just before its removal in the mid 1980s. Masts were jig built and soldered up from correct profile brass lengths of varying section. The compound catenary wires were built in-situ using nickel-silver wire. This was developed from pioneering techniques used at the Riverside MRC at Tilbury, who built model West Coast electrification in the late 1970s. The positions of the masts and the track plan on Deepcar were derived from a layout plan supplied by BR.

The EM2s are rebuilt *Triang Hornby* items, which for a product of the 1960s are remarkably good. The EM1s are resin kits powered for the most part by *Lima* mechanisms. A few are white metal, one or two *Olivias Trains* Class 76s have recently joined the fleet, and a vintage Trix product is an occasional guest. The first model engines we built are now as old as the real ones were in 1980, and many have clocked up very considerable mileages. Layout control is analogue with section switches - there was no DCC in the 1980s. The majority of rolling stock is kit-built, again because very little appropriate ready-to-run stock was around when it was created. When we started exhibiting the layout, it featured the original EM1 and EM2 classes, and was set in the early 1960s. We found however there was more demand for the corporate blue era, and that is the form in which the layout is now presented at exhibitions.

Other excellent layouts featuring the Woodhead Route have appeared over the years but Deepcar continues to be the only large exhibition layout in 00 to feature working DC overhead. One of the original Builders went on to create his own equally unique 7mm (0 Gauge) portrayal, Netherwood Sidings, and even developed his own etched brass and resin kit for an EM1. Many of the Deepcar builders have since followed suit and built O Gauge Class 76s.

(left) **The station at Deepcar showing the superb catenary and attention to detail.**

A double-headed Merry-Go-Round coal train with a pair of 76s. Deepcar has a fleet of about twenty locomotives, including half a dozen pre-TOPS engines, and the prototype, E26000 TOMMY.

Not a model this one but an actual 76 headlight (top of cab) which was salvaged by one of the NMRS members and restored back to working order. Rumour has it that a full size bogie is now on the drawing board!

76053 and MU-fitted 76007 on the 7mm scale offshoot 'Netherwood Sidings' created by Graham Clark. Graham wanted so many Class 76s to operate the trains on his layout that he decided to produce his own etched kit. To help spread the cost Graham produced more kits than the layout needed, and members of the NMRS purchased the extra ones from him. Graham has also produced a scratch built EM2 in 7mm scale.

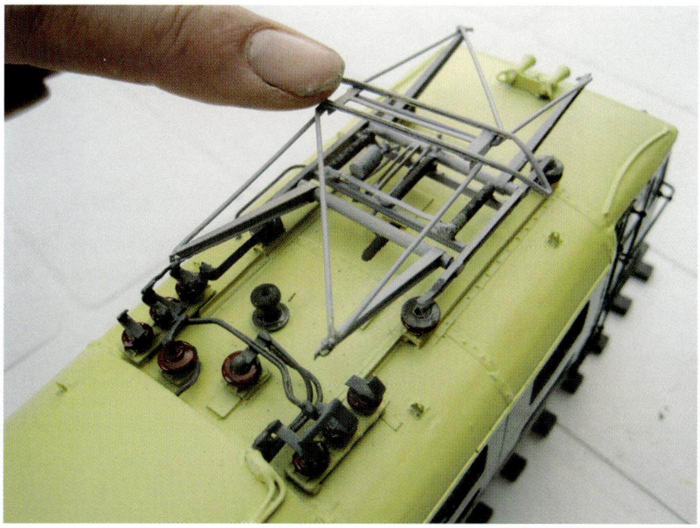

(clockwise from above) **Pantograph detail on one of the 7mm models. And they work. Incredible! Two 76s or are they EM1s? in the making. The majority of NMRS members who have constructed Graham Clark's kits have plumped for the TOPS version. Only one went for the green-era. However, they all went for the twin-motors option, and working lights. Dave Paylor working on his 76 at a club night. A view of Netherwood Sidings during its debut at Nottingham in 2011. Heading a coal train is 76025.**

E26057 ULYSSES in that glorious lined green finish. This 7mm scale model was built by Hayden Reed using a kit produced by Graham Clark. Hayden has yet to pluck up enough courage to weather it! *(below)* **This 7mm scale model of 76051 built by Geoff Brain features door handles which actually work! The cab layout is apparently so good that we cannot publish a picture in case it frightens people off.**

HOPEFULLY THIS BOOK HAS INSPIRED YOU TO TAKE UP MODELLING THE MSW AND ITS LOCOMOTIVES. IF YOU WANT ANY ADVICE ON ANY ASPECT OF THE LINE THEN GET IN TOUCH WITH THE PEOPLE AT NMRS THEY WOULD BE HAPPY TO HEAR FROM YOU..